AGRO'S GARDENING SERIES

BONSAI

An Art of Minature Plant Culture

S. C. DEY

AGROBIOS (INDIA)

Published by:
Agrobios (India)
Agro House, Behind Nasrani Cinema
Chopasani Road, Jodhpur - 342 002
Phone: 91-0291-2642319, Fax: 2643993
E. mail: agrobios@sify.com

ISBN : 978-81-7754-122-6 *(Bonsai HB)*

ISBN : 978-81-7754-351-3 *(Bonsai PB)*

9 788177 541229
Rs. 1395.00 / US$ .00
Published by:
AGROBIOS (INDIA)

Published by: **Updesh Purohit for Agrobios (India), Jodhpur**
Lasertypeset at: **Yashee Computers, Jodhpur**
Cover Design by: **Reena**
Printed at: **Babloo Offset, Jodhpur**

Preface

The practice of growing plants in pots led to grow bonsai. The herbs and shrubs are grown extensively in containers. Occasionally tree species were tried in pots. They, however, could not grow tall as they do in nature. As the time passed away they gradually got the imprints of age that made them more beautiful and caught the imagination of growers and viewers alike. It is then the impetus to bonsai growing generated. Gradually it began to spread to the different parts of the globe. Many techniques were innovated and applied, which were the artificial means for giving the natural touches to the bonsai. The imprints of age is brought about earlier than usual. Hence the utility of the techniques.

Bonsai growing is developed into a special branch of home gardening. Bonsai is grown with love and affection which is comparable to rearing pets. It demands more care and attention to attain perfection.

Bonsai culture was innovated in China and developed in Japan. It is held in great esteem by the Japanese and associated gradually with their culture. Century-old bonsai are not the rare things there. The art and science of growing bonsai are taught to the members of the bonsai societies of Japan.House plants are beautiful for their attractive foliage whereas bonsai are for their age-old grotesque form. Both are reared as indoor plants. If a good number of bonsai are grown a conservatory is needed to accommodate them. The old and disabled who cannot take part in normal gardening can devote their efforts to bonsai growing. A bonsai passes from generation to generation. That is why a specimen bonsai is older than the existing generations-new as well as old. Bonsai growing lends itself well to immense joy of creation, and a specimen work remains to be a curio for generation after generation. The market value of an attractive bonsai can hardly be ascertained. In this regard it is comparable to an age-old masterpiece of an able sculptor.

The containers for bonsai are of special type. Even today these are not available extensively. They are procurable from the cities. On account of the dearth of ground space for gardening the city dwellers are bound to take up pot culture. For this reason the population of pot plants are more in the cities. So the pots of all descriptions are available there. The pots for the dicots and monocots are different. The pots for the later should be narrow at the top in comparison with the bottom. Because the excessive root growth at the bottom may push the soil ball out of the pot. The narrow mouth of the pot prevents the soil ball from coming out.

The book is designed for those who are eager to have the guidance and instructions for growing their own bonsai. Even those who purchase bonsai or semi-bonsai from the bonsai nursery invariably need the guidance for rearing their subjects.

To make the text attractive and interpretative as many as 150 figures have been included in the text. All the line drawings have been drawn by the author himself. An acknowledgement expressing gratitude to the persons concerned is included. They have assisted in providing photographs and transparencies for illustration. More than 30 books on gardening have been published in his credit. Thousands of readers are in praise of the works and insisted him on writing a book on bonsai. This encouragement prompted him to write this book on bonsai. If it is found useful to the bonsai growers the efforts of the author as well as those who are concerned with the bringing out the book will be worthwhile.

Horticultural Arena **S.C. Dey**
Jhargram Pin 721507

Acknowledgements

I am glad to express my deep gratitude and obligation to those who helped me immensely in preparing the manuscript including the graphic materials - figures and photographs. Of them Mr. Anal Ghosh and Mr. Basab Datta figures prominently. Mr. Ghosh, an able bonsai specialist kindly agreed and permitted me to take snaps of his treasure in the form of age-old minature trees. Mr. Datta with his love of nature and dexterity in photography helped in the transfer of those individuals of the grotesque form from the garden to the printed page of the book.

I am also thankful to Dr. S. S. Purohit who with his immense knowledge in the sphere of publication of agro-botanical literatures justifiably suggested to me to prepare an exhaustive manuscript on bonsai.

Contents

1. Group Planting, as if a grove CV : *Tamarindus indica*
2. Forest Style, CV : *Murraya paniculata*
3. Formal Upright style (not trained) CV : *Commiphora mukul*
4. Group Planting
5. 'Trio' grown on flat rock. CV : *Ficus nuda*
6. Umbrella Style, CV : *Ficus nuda*
7. Bamboo clan in concrete pot (Monocot)
8. Rock-Grown, CV : *Ficus nuda*(Courtesy : Asim Nanda Das)
9. Rock-Grown, CV : *Ficus retusa*
10. Bonsai of Bougainvillea, Adenium and *P. afra*
11. Group Planting, CV : *Ficus nuda*
12. Group Planting, CV : *Tamarindus indica*
13. Informal Upright Style, CV : *Pinus longifolia*
14. Umbrella Style, CV : *Portulacaria afra*
15. Formal Upright Style, CV : *Tamarindus indica*
16. Bamboo Clean (Monocot)
17. Umbrella Style
18. A unique Style of *Portulacaria afra*
19. *Ficus bengalensis* with a good number of prop roots.
20. Mulberry in a Slanting Style (Grown by the author)
21. Date Palm (Monocot) in a bare-root condition to show the root growth (Grown by the author)
22. Plumeria (Grown by the author)
23. *Ficus bengalensis* bearing ripe fruits in plenty (Grown by the author)
24. Bonsai of miniature rose, Umbrella Style.

Introduction

India has mainly three types of climatic conditions, such as tropical, subtropical and temperate. Certain vallies of the Himalayas, however, have very cold weather where the delicate garden plants have to be protected from the snowfall for a couple of months in winter. From the peninsular region of the country to the snow – clad vallies of the Himalayas the temperature variation is considerable. Therefore the cultural practices relating to the climatic conditions vary. It is obvious that the extreme climates, i.e. too hot or too cold are harmful to bonsai culture.

The extreme sun in summer is not conducive. Therefore a conservatory that helps control the intensity of sun and heat as well as the level of humidity is necessary to make the bonsai culture easy. The construction of conservatories has been dealt with in a separate chapter.

Bonsai is grown in the shallow pots with the minimum of soil, sometimes on rocks and bricks. So the pot soil may dry up quickly that entails frequent watering. To ensure the supply of moisture especially in the extremely dry and hot weather automatic watering system should be introduced. During the absence of all members of the family for holidaying the bonsai pots can be watered in the same way. The capillary system of watering or drip system by plastic tubing can be adopted with advantage. These processes have been explained with the suitable illustrations in the relevant chapter.

Ageing is the prime factor of making a good bonsai. The imprints of age from top to bottom makes it grotesque but beautiful. Animals are hardly beautiful in their old age.

On the contrary the aged plants are more beautiful than their early stage. Hence the importance of bonsai. The plants, unlike animals, do not lose their fecundity due to age. So an age-old bonsai can bear flowers and fruits that can be an added attraction.

A specimen bonsai bears the deep imprint of age. But more it is sculptured than natural. The techniques of sculpture in plants have to be learnt by the bonsai maker. The beauty of a bonsai is directly related to its sculptural quality. Sculpturing involves in shaping and making the imprints of deep suffering.

Why Bonsai

Practically bonsai growing was started since the gardener attempted to grow plants in pots. The love for plants intrigued them to enjoy nature more intimately. They aspired to have plants like many household belongings or pets. Therefore the plant lovers desired to grow plants among them. This longing for indoor plants led to innovate pot culture.

It is said that a Chainese poet named Guen-ming on his retirement from the government service took to growing chrysanthemums in pots before 400 B.C. He reared the plants in the verandah of the house. Perhaps he was the first, who used pots for growing plants. In course of time the bonsai growing developed from the pot culture of plants. It was innovated in the sixth century. Many oil paintings during the reign of T'ang dynesty represent the bonsai of pine, cypress, plum, bamboo etc. Bonsai growing has been mingled with the culture of the Chinese. Sustained efforts of centuries enabled the Japanese to innovate the technique of making bonsai of the tree species. The term *BONSAI* is derived from the Japanese language meaning a tree in a plate, i.e. the miniature form of a tree grown in a plate-like shallow pot. A typical specimen should not exceed 70cm in height and be dwarfer than 20cm.

The principle in bonsai culture of the East and West are not the same, i.e. two different trends in very conception are apparent. The idea of the West in this regard is very simple. Because bonsai to them is everything of an age-old tree excepting its prodigious height.

In the East bonsai, brilliant in its conception inspired the Zen Buddhists to meditation. They believed in the conception of simplicity, naturalness and asymmetry in every object of nature and are used to laying importance on the useful and discarding the others. They are interested in bringing about the harmony between man and nature, and as such a bonsai is regarded as a religious object that help them to be absorbed in meditation.

The question arises, is bonsai a fruit-bearing tree, flowering plant or a foliage ornamental ? It should merely be an ornamental. However in choosing species for making a bonsai one has liberty to use shrubs or trees that may or may not be noted for their flower or fruit. It a bonsai becomes attractive with beautiful flowers or fruits that is regarded as an added quality or attraction. Practically the bonsai is a miniature form of a giant tree that bears the imprints of age with assymetrical grotesque style.

Aesthetic Aspects

Both the art of sculpture and the science of horticulture should go hand-in-hand to make a successful bonsai. If one falls short of the amount required the preponderance of the other cannot compensate it. So maintaining balance is also an art that derives from the sense of proportion. It is rightly said that a bonsai is a piece of living sculpture.

Horticulture the science of growing garden plants contributes to the lively growth of the bonsai and the art of sculpture lends itself to the artistically grotesque shape. The plant parts including the roots, trunk, branches, leaves, flowers and fruits are properly groomed to present a combined effect lending itself to beauty characteristic of nature alone. In shaping the frame work or structure the balance has to be wrought. Here, however, 'balance' has no literal meaning. It will be brought out laying emphasis on asymmetry. So it is a word of the terminology of the discipline. The implication of 'balance' lies in that it follows a definite rule. The growth of the branches (vertical and lateral) though assymetrical should form a triangle. The triangle symbolizes god, man and earth. The top angle stands for god. The lateral branches in the middle represent man and the basal branches the earth. Another interpretation after *Vedanta* is the *Sat-Chit-Ananda,* the characteristics of *Brahma*, the creator of the universe. *Brahma* is regarded as the eternal source of wisdome and joy, Hence 'Sachhidananda'.

Details of Bonsai Parts

It is obvious that from the root to fruit a bonsai is the imitation of an age old tree. The details of the different arts are discussed here with a view to improving their appearance conforming to the bonsai-like style. The defects, general or specific, are pointed out so that one can proceed to attain perfection.

ROOT

The root has two purposes – to provide anchorage and absorb chemical nutrients with water. Without good anchorage a tree cannot stand erect. In nature those trees which are inclined lack balanced root system. If they do not grow proportionately in all directions run the risk of blowing over by storms or get inclined. Soil erosion in one side may also be the cause of a inclined trunk. The trees growing near the water course may tilt towards the water.

The tall trees develop a thick and long tap root which passes deep into the soil straight. This root alone gives a very strong anchorage. If the soil is not deep enough the tap root cannot grow long. The presence of the layer of shallow stone or *murram* in the sub - soil makes the soil layer shallow. Obviously a bonsai in a shallow pot cannot grow its tap root. On the contrary the lateral roots become thicker. The thick roots just above the soil surface are the characteristic of a aged tree. So the bonsai grower should be mindful in this respect. In other wards, his bonsai must have the thick roots partly or fully exposed. Their formation should be like the claw of a bird, i.e. nearly symmetrical. Uniformly spreading roots seen above the soil look nice and suitable

for formal, informal and slanting styles. The most of the mangrove plants have exposed roots. In the region of light soil many old trees are found to stand on their thick exposed roots due to the gradual process of soil erosion. So to imitate nature the bonsai growers artificially make their plants of such appearance although the plants look insecure.

If the roots are not seen above the soil the trees trunk looks a pole inserted in the ground. To make the lateral roots exposed the shallow planting at the time of repotting is recommended. The soil above the rim level of the pot will gradually be eroded by watering. All the thick roots remain exposed when the plants are grown on the blocks of stone or bricks.

TIPS

1. If the roots grow straight place them horizontally while repotting. The thicker portion of the horizontal roots should be above the rim level. Generally it is not done in the early stage. Because it does not become necessary until the roots become thick.

2. If the development of roots is not symmetrical, i.e. forming a gap in one side scrape the point deep up to the cambium layer with a sharp knife. Treat the cut surface with a contact fungicide and then cover the operated portion with sphagnum moss, mixed with soil. Keep the moss moist, the new roots will grow within a few weeks, which will be thicker in course of time.

3. Another process is to make a hole at the point where a root is required. The tool like a hand drill can be used to make the hole. Apply any suitable root hormone powder in the hole and fill it with sand and cover the area with soil as usual. New roots will sprout within a few weeks.

TRUNK

Thick and grotesque trunk representing a particular form is pleasing to the viewers. Very old specimen must bear the marks of suffering. Generally they are seen on the trunk.

The trunk-line represents a particular style. The presence of rough and rugged barks contributes to the marks of age. The thick trunk with spreading roots at the base on the soil surface shows the rigidity and stability of a tree acquired through decades. Sometimes the spreading branches are not so thick to proportionate the thickness of the trunk. Not only the trunk should be thick but the spreading branches also should be thick proportionately. Sometimes attempts are made to lift the large plants from the ground, the trunk is cut across and potted to make a bonsai overnight. A number of branches grow just below the transversely cut end. But this process of making bonsai is wrong. The exception is however, found in the case of plumerias. I made experiments with the species and become successful to make a curio.

Though the graceful body contours make the bonsai beautiful too many zigzag curves on the trunk are not desirable. The conspicuous marks of cuts due to faulty pruning are also unsightly.

BRANCHES

Not only shortening but also shaping of branches have to be made artificially. In nature the old trees having crooked branches in the criss-cross way are common. But in making bonsai branches are trained to grow in a simple way. They should not be made too much crooked. Because anything in excess is sure to lose balance resulting in an eyesore.

There are a number of popular styles any of them is followed while training a bonsai. All of them have been discussed with illustration exclusively in a chapter.

FOLIAGE

Foliage soften the rugged structure of the branches as flesh covers the frame work of bones or garments beautify the body. Foliage along with the branching system defines the outlines of a plant so also that of a bonsai. Good foliage for bonsai should be fresh, green and compact, and the individual leaves must be small. For making it more attractive with tender and glossy foliage the showman follows a technique of defoliating the bonsai nearly six weeks before the show date. The pruning of leaves forces to sprout the new leaves. Leaf pruning is also adopted for reducing the leaf size of the bonsai. In case of old plants it is found to be successful. If necessitated it should be done once a year only. It should be borne in mind that leaf pruning weakens the plant. So it should not be practised recklessly. The size of flower and fruit, however, cannot be reduced by leaf pruning.

Indoor Bonsai

The different tree species of the tropical and subtropical parts of the world are very suitable for making bonsai. Even in cold countries the tropical species are used for this purpose. Obviously they need the greenhouse omission extremely cold weather the greenhouse is heated to provide warmth necessary for the plants of the tropical climates. Hence the significance of the name *Indoor Bonsai*. Paul Lessniwick has published a book which is titled *Indoor Bonsai* (1985). Even in the tropical or subtropical climates bonsai are reared in a semi-shade condition especially in summer. So bonsai pots are kept in the conservatory, verandah or window-sills. Virtually our bonsai are also grown indoors. Instead of the greenhouse they need conservatory. In a separate chapter the construction of the conservatory has been dealt with.

INTENSITY OF LIGHT

In our country rearing of bonsai is not practised within the room as is done in the West. There artificial lighting is resorted to. Because the direct sun light or any substitute is essentially required for carbon assimilation by the green leaves. This process is a must for manufacturing plant food principally the carbohydrates. Carbon from the carbon dioxide of the atmosphere is absorbed through the leaf-pores and are used as a raw material of the products.

The exposure to the direct sun for the most part of the day is found not conducive to bonsai growing. Hence the need of a light shade. Fibre-glass shed is highly suitable for the most bonsai. Fibre-glass sheets are not perfectly transparent rather translucent. In the old shed only 30-35 percent light is available. Because on ageing their translucency increases. Even grown inside the room the light intensity should necessarily be 200-1000 lux. The lux being the unit of measuring the light intensity.

Ideal Environments For Bonsai

Miniature trees, like house plants, grow indoors. Yet the house cannot be their natural environment. It can be regarded as a tolerable substute. Because the influence of day and night, seasonal changes, humidity and dryness of air go a long way to effect the physiological changes in the plant body for their perfect growth and production. Therefore, they should be reared in the natural environment. But they must be protected from the extreme climatic conditions. For this reason the environment of a conservatory can be suitable to a great extent. Its environment lies in between the entirely outdoor or indoor conditions.

Now a days the conservatories of any size can be erected in no time by using agro-shade nets which are made of plastic like materials and available in all cities of the country. They are made in the different grades to adjust all sorts of light requirements in the different seasons. In winter the miniature trees need more light. Obviously it is opposite in summer.

The light filters through the net to permeate the house. By the use of different grades of the netting 50-75 percent of the direct sun can be available inside the conservatory. The netting is fixed horizontally as a canopy over a structure of bamboo or wooden laths. On the sides the netting is fixed vertically that corresponds to the walls. In the coastal regions coconut leaves are conveniently used to make a conservatory. Previously bamboo laths or wooden slats were used for this purpose. In this process two inch wide strips

of bamboo or wood are placed side by side with a gap of one inch in between. In summer this gap is reduced by placing the strips closely. In case of the canopy of agro-shade rets the thin netting are replaced by the thick ones which filter the less sun.

To accommodate a good number of shade-loving foliage plants a conservatory is necessary. The bonsai and other indoor plants are housed in the same conservatory. A lean-to-the house conservatory of the required dimensions is erected close to the house. Occasionally for the decoration or display purpose the miniature trees are brought from the conservatory.

The tropical plants are accustomed to grow in high temperatures. Most of them shed their leaves completely or partially in winter because of their deciduous habit and remain dormant for few months until the temperature rises in spring. On the high altitudes where the climate is temperate the miniature trees need to be reared in 'hot houses' where the day temperature goes below 16°C (60°F). Because the temperature ranging from 18-24°C (64-75°F) is ideal for their growth. The high temperature extending upto 36°C is also tolerable for them.

If the temperate plant species are reared in the subtropical climates they should be sheltered from the high temperature and hot wind. Pine, juniper, rhododendron etc. are put in this group. Pine, juniper and certain magnolias are, however, readily acclimatized to subtropical conditions. The cool conservatory having the deffused sun and humidified with a mist sprinkler can be a good shelter in summer for the bonsai of the temperate species.

Selection of Species

A wide range of tropical trees and shrubs can be the materials for creating bonsai. As the herbaceous plants are not woody cannot be used for this purpose. The climbing shrubs are hardly used for this purposes. The monocots like palms and cycas can be the planting materials for bonsai. The following species have been grouped on the basis of their utility or uses. The species for bonsai should have the following characteristics.

1. It should be hardy to stand the hardships during training.
2. Those which manifest the marks of ageing earlier than usual.
3. The species having rough and dark coloured trunk.
4. The branching system and branches are attractive. The branches of crooked form are desirable.
5. The roots round the base of the trunk that grow horizontally near the surface soil become thick early.
6. The shoots having short internodes.
7. The species with the habit of growing aerial roots as in Ficus.
8. Leaves are small that grow thickly.
9. Evergreen or deciduous. The semi-deciduous species are not liked.
10. Having small flowers of brillant colours.

A

The plants of this group are deciduous. They shed their all leaves in winter and remain dormant for few months. With the rise in temperature in spring they put forth new leaves. Generally blossom is followed by foliage. They are mainly propagated by seed.

Adansonia digitata

Family : *Bombacaceae*

Other names : Eng.-Baobab, Monkey bread tree, Hindi-Gorakh imli, Lichora

Its native place is tropical Africa. The trunk is extremely thick in comparison with the height of the plants. It has a similarity with the silk-cotton tree. Both the plants belong to the same family. It is propagated by seed.

Fig. 1: *Adansonia digitata*

Azadirachta indica

Family : *Meliaceae*

Other names : Eng.– Margosa tree, Neem tree; Hindi and Beng. Nim.

It is a very popular tree which bears small sweet scented flowers in March-April. The foliage is very ornamental. *Neem* is grown as an avenue tree. Fruits ripe in June. On sowing seeds germinate well. The viability of seed remains for a few months only.

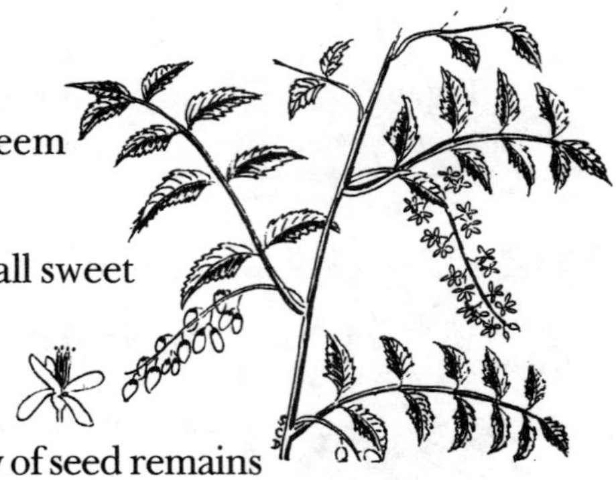

Fig. 2: *Azadirachta indica*

Bassia latifolia

Family : *Sapotaceae*

Other names : Eng. – Illipe butter; Hindi and Beng. – Mohua.

The tree is large, which grows in the forest. Leaves are large. The flowers are bead-like and transluscent. Dry flowers are used in distilling country wine. The plant is propagated by seed.

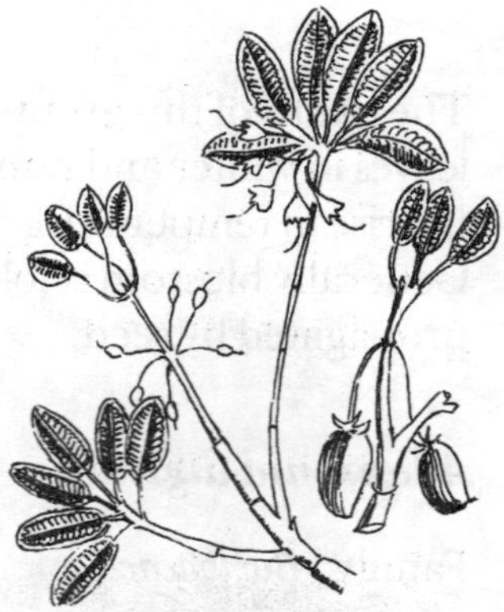

Fig. 3:
Bassia latifolia

Fig. 4:
Butea monosperma

Butea monosperma

Family : *Papilionaceae*

Other names : Eng. Flame of the forest ; Hindi-Dhak ; Beng. – Palas.

A small deciduous tree. Leaves are large and shaggy It is a flowering tree. The bonsai of this species may produce flowers. The flowering season being March and April. The plants are grown from seed or suckers.

Fig. 5:
Cassia fistula

Cassia fistula

Family : *Caesalpiniaceae*

Other names : Eng. – Golden shower, Indian laburnum, Purging Cassia, Hindi – Amaltas.

The species is wild in the most part of the country. It is extensively grown in parks and avenues. Leaves are compounds and large. Fruits are like a baton. The plant is multiplied by seed.

Commiphora mukul

Family : *Burseraceae*

Other names : Eng. – Indian bdellium tree ; Hindi-Guggul; Beng. –Guggul.

It is a plant of dry region of the country. Fragrant gum-resin know as gum-guggual obtained from the bark is used as an incense and as a fixative in perfumery.

A cutting of the pencil thickness can be grown to a bonsai within three years. So it is an ideal material for the beginners.

Diospyros exsculpta

Family : *Ebenaceae*

Other names : Nepal ebony, Persimmon ; Hindi-Kendu.

It grows in the wild. Its leaves are used in wrapping *bidis*. Leaves are large. The plant is propagated by seed or sucker.

Ficus religiosa

Family : *Moraceae*

Other names : Eng. Peepul, Bo-tree, Hindi-Pipal ; Beng.-Asvattha.

A sacred tree of Hindus and Buddhists. It is widely used for making a mini bonsai in a cup-like pot. Seedlings are found to grow from the air borne seeds in the crevices of the walls. The seedlings can be raised by sowing seeds on a special type of compost (See next Chapter)

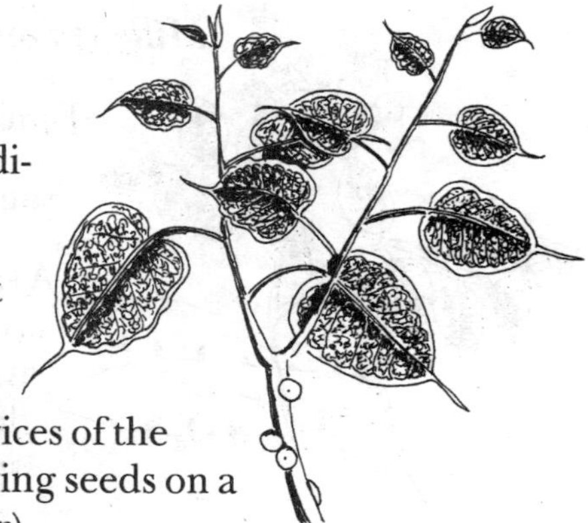

Fig. 6:
Ficus religiosa

Lagerstroemia speciosa

Family : *Lythraceae*

Leaves are large and flowers are mauve. The branching system is compact and the head is symmetrical. The seeds are large, which germinate well from March-July.

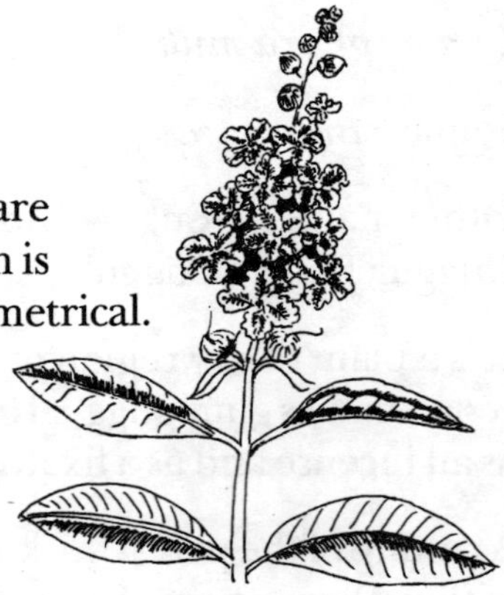

Fig. 7:
Lagerstroemia speciosa

Legerstroemia thorelli

It is a dwarf species. The bonsai of this larger stroemia is found to be more floriferous. The species is a tree of medium height, which is quite different from the shrub Lagerstroemias.

Millettia ovalifolia.

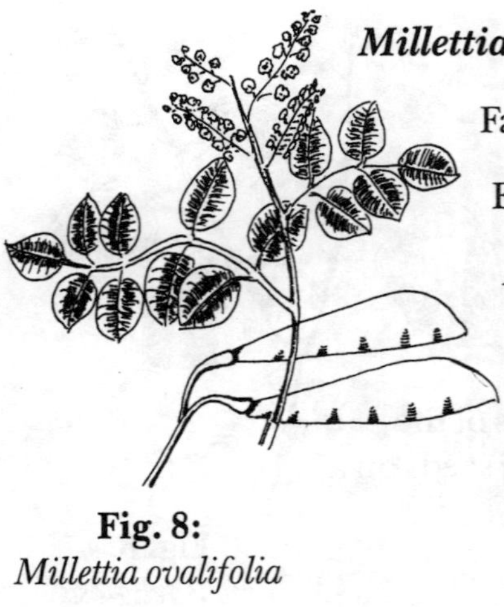

Fig. 8:
Millettia ovalifolia

Family : *Papilionaceae*

English name : Moulmein rosewood

A small tree of compound leaves. Leaflets are large and oval. It is grown as an avenue tree. In summer the plant is decked with blue flowers. It is a good species for bonsai. The plant is propagated easily by seed.

Terminalia arjuna

Family : *Combretaceae*

Other names : Eng. – Arjuna ; Hindi-Arjun, Maruthu, Kuhu.

The tree is found in most part of country and also grown as an avenue tree. Leaves are medium. The branches are flexible, hence suitable for bonsai training. The fruits collected in summer should be sown in June-July.

Fig. 9:
Terminalia arjuna

Terminalia bellirica

Family : *Combretaceae*

Other names : Eng. – Belleric myrobalan, Bastard myrobalan, Hindi- Bahera, Vibhitaka.

A common tree growing throughout the deciduous forest of the country and also grown as an avenue tree. Leaves are large and oval. The seed coat is very hard. So a seed takes few months to germinate.

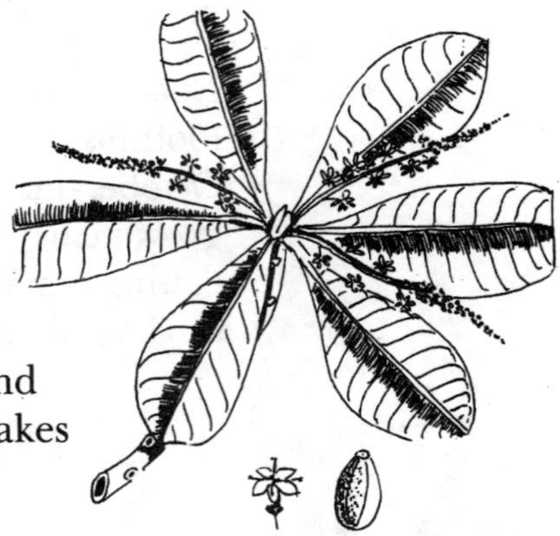

Fig. 10:
Terminalia bellirica

B

This group includes the semi-deciduous trees. In winter the leaves become sparse. Obviously this group of plants lies between the deciduous and the evergreen. The plant to be exhibited in winter shows must have their full foliage or be leafless. So the plants of this group are not suitable for this purpose.

Anacardium occidentale

Family : *Anacardiaceae*

Other names : Eng. – Cashrew ; Hindi and Beng. – Kaju.

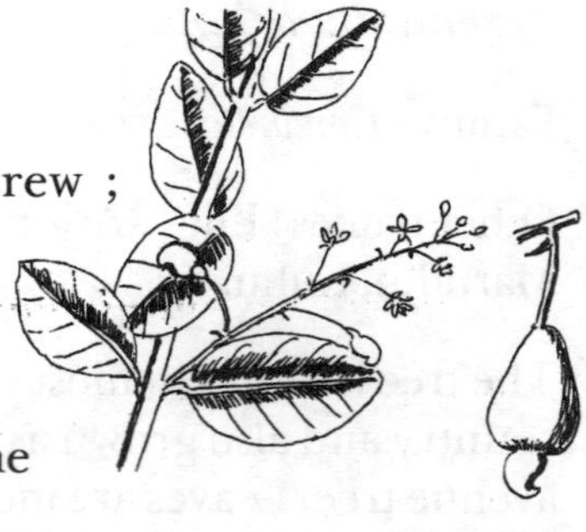

Fig. 11: *Anacardium occidentale*

Native to tropical America. It is grown extensively on sand dunes of the coastal region. The tree is very popular for the delicious nuts. The plant is propagated by seed or air layering. The seeds should be sown within a few weeks of harvest.

Bauhinia purpurea

Family : *Caesalpiniaceae*

Other names : Eng. – Camel's foot tree, Pink Bauhinia, Hindi-Kaliar, Lal Kachnar ; Beng.-Lal Kanchan.

Native to India. It grows abundantly in the slopes and the foothills of the Himalayas. The flowering season being October-January. The plant grows fast, so a bonsai can be grown early. It is propagated by seed or cuttings. Thick cuttings strike well. So a plant grown from a thick cutting can be trained to a bonsai earlier than the usual process.

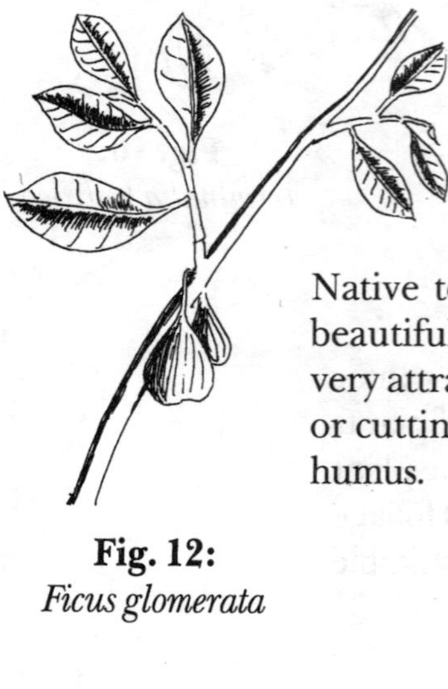

Fig. 12: *Ficus glomerata*

Ficus glomerata

Family : *Moraceae*

Other names : Eng.-Cluster fig ; Hindi-Gular, Domeer, Beng-Jajnadomoor.

Native to India. The trees are of medium height and beautiful. Leaves are large, glossy. Fruits are round and very attractive when ripe. The plant is propagated by seed or cuttings. Seeds should be sown in the compost rich in humus.

Gardenia latifolia

Family : Rubiaceae

Other names : Eng.-Box-wood Gardenia ; Hindi-Papra, Paphar ; Beng.-Bon pindalu ; Santal-Bhudru.

Native to India. It grows in the deciduous forest of the laterite soil. Leaves are large, flowers are white fragrant. The bark is thick and the wood is pliable hence ideal for training. The plant is propagated by seed or air layering.

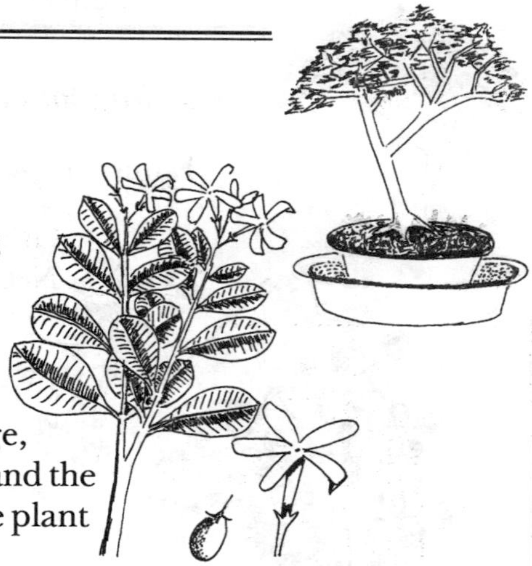

Fig. 13:
Gardenia latifolia

Gravillea robusta

Family : *Proteaceae*

Other names : Eng.-Silver oak, Silky oak.

Native to Australia. A large robust tree of fern – like ornamental foliage. The plant is grown in gardens and road sides. The plant is propagated by seed.

Fig. 14:
Gravillea robusta

Michelia alba

Family : *Magnoliaceae*

Other names : Eng.-Champac ; Hindi-Champa ; Beng.- Swet Champa.

Native to India. Leaves are glossy. It flowers through all seasons but in large quantities from March-October. The plant is vegetatively propagated by inarching or veneer grafting.

Millingtonia hortinsis

Family : *Bignoniaceae*

Other names : Eng.-Indian Cork tree ; Hindi-Neem Chemeli, Akash neem ; Beng.-Seetahar.

Native to India. Very tall tree, cultivated throughout India. It is very popular as an avenue tree. Leaves are very ornamental. Flowers are white and fragrant. The plant is propagated by seed or sucker.

Fig. 15:
Millingtonia hortinsis

Fig. 16:
Polyalthia longifolia

Polyalthia longifolia

Family : *Annonaceae*

Other names : Eng.-Mast tree ; Hindi-Kudumi, Asokan Beng.-Debdaru.

The tree is slender. So very suitable for landscaping with group planting. The plant is propagated from seeds that germinate well. The viability of seed lasts for a few weeks only.

Saraca indica

Family : *Caesalpiniaceae*

Other name : Eng.-Asoke tree; Hindi - Ashok, Ampich; Beng. - Ashok.

Native to India. It is grown in gardens as a good flowering tree. Leaves are large, compound and drooping. Flowers of orange colour come up in large bunches. The plant is propagated by seed. Seeds are very large, which germinate readily on sowing within a few weeks of harvesting.

Fig. 17:
Saraca indica

Tabebuia palida

Family : *Bignoniaceae*.

The plant is grown along the road sides. The flowers are white with a tinge of lilac. Leaves are glossy and ornamental. The plant is propagated by seed.

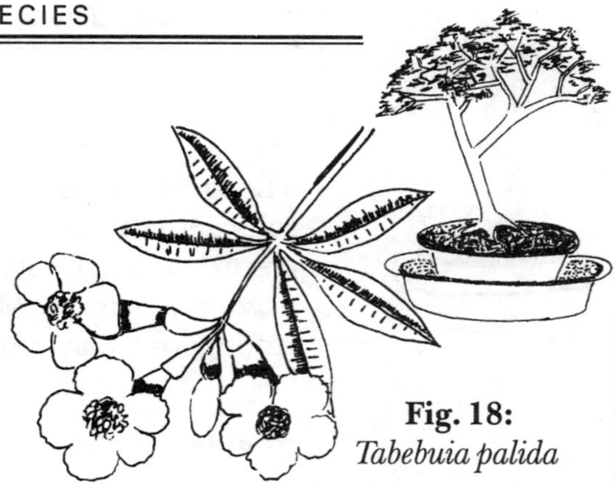

Fig. 18: *Tabebuia palida*

Tecoma gaudi chaudi

Family : *Bignoniaceae*

Other names : Eng.-Yellow elder, yellow Bells; Beng.-Gauri-Chori.

It is a large shrub or small tree of ornamental gardens. The plant bears bright yellow flowers for a number of times in a year. Leaves are large, coarse and compound. The plant is propagated from seeds or air-layering.

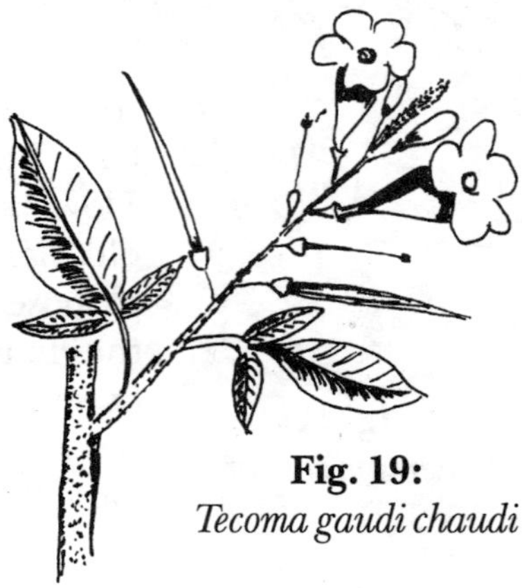

Fig. 19: *Tecoma gaudi chaudi*

Thespesia populnea

Family : *Malvaceae*

Other names : Eng.-Portia tree ; Hindi-Paraspipal ; Beng.-Paras.

Native to India. A common tree of the coastal region. The stem is gnarled and grotesque. Leaves are large and heart-shaped. Flowers are like hibiscus. Colour is yellow turning bronze next day. It is grown as an avenue tree. Fruits are abundant that contain a good number of seeds. Plant are grown easily from seed.

Fig. 20: *Thespesia populnea*

C

This group of plants are shrubs which may be erect or subscandent. Some climbers are grown like a perfect shrub in gardens, e.g. Bougainvillea, Uvaria, *Artabotrys odoratissimus*, *Petrea volubilis* etc. Most shrubs are easily propagated by cuttings or air layering.

Adenium obesum

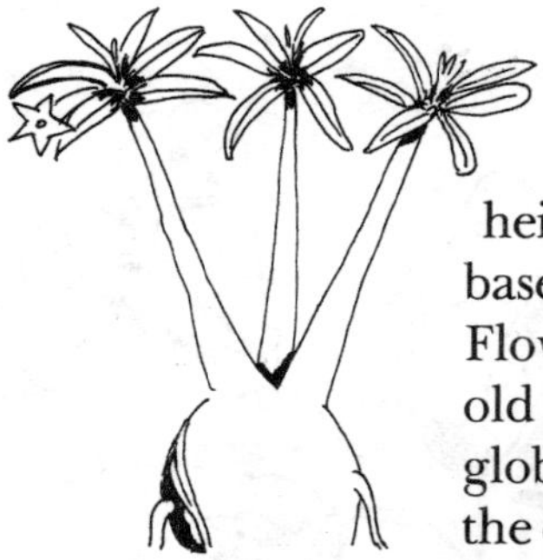

Fig. 21: *Adenium obesum*

Family : *Apocynaceae*

A very popular shrub growing up to 2.5 metres in height in heavy soils. Its stem is succulent with a globose base. The leaves are in cluster at the top of the branches. Flowers are white with a tinge of pinkish crimson. The old plants without any training look like a bonsai. The globose base and the thick roots above the soil level are the characteristics of the plant. The plant is propagated by seed or cuttings. The viability of seed is very short, i.e. for a few weeks only. Sow seed immediately on harvest.

Caesalpinia pulcherrima

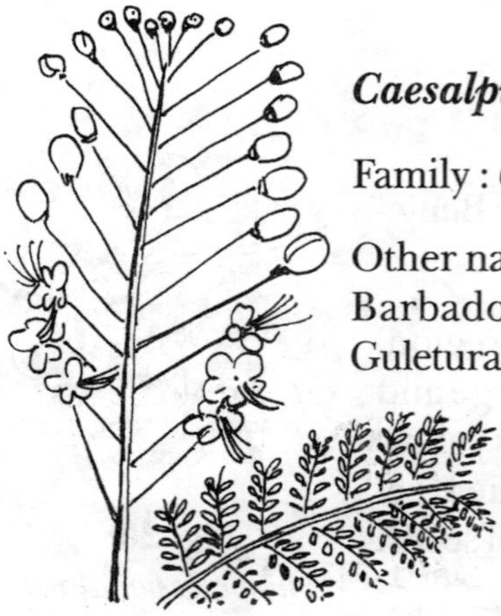

Fig. 22: *Caesalpinia pulcherrima*

Family : *Caesalpiniaceae*

Other names : Beng.-Krishnachura, Eng.-Peacock flower, Barbados pride, Paradise flower ; Hindi-Gul-mohur Guletura.

A bushy shrub that grows well without any care. Like Gulmohar its leaves are feathery. Its shoot terminated with a bunch of orange scarlet flowers. The plant is propagated by seed.

Calliandra sps

Family : *Mimosaceae*

English name : Power puff.

The genus 'Calliandra' has a number of species, most of them are ornamental and grown in gardens. The leaves are feather-like. Only one species has few broad leaflets. Flowers are like the powder puff. The bright coloured stamens (Male organs) are numerous, large and attractive. The petals are not conspicuous. The plants are easily propagated by seed or air layering.

Duranta repens.

Family : *Verbanaceae*

Other names : Eng.-Golden dew drop, Pigeon berry ; Beng.-Doranta.

This shrub is used as a hedge plant for the garden compound. The plant is evergreen with ornamental foliage. The attractive blue flowers and orange berries are the added attraction of the plant. It is propagated easily by soft or hard cuttings in the rains. Seeds germinate with difficulty.

Hibiscus rosa-sinensis

Family : *Malvaceae*

Other names : Eng.-Shoe flower ; Hindi-Gulhar, Jasum.

A typical evergreen shrub with very ornamental and large flowers. The plant easily propagated by soft or hard cuttings or air layering. The modern Hawaiian varieties are multiplied by bud grafting.

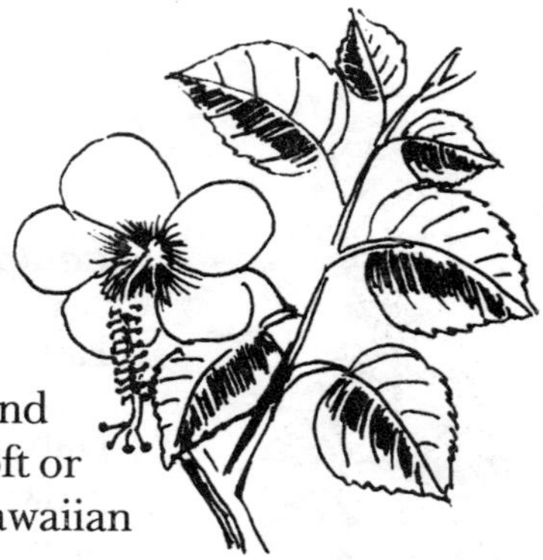

Fig. 23:
Hibiscus rosa-sinensis

Jatropha *sps.*

Family : *Euphorbiaceae*

A shrub or small tree. *J. curcas* is a large shrub. But *J. podagrica* is a small shrub. It looks like an Adenium. The most species are the native to tropical America. The plant is succulent that contains an transparent latex. Its stem is like those of Guggul, Plumeria etc. The plant is propagated by seed or cuttings.

Fig. 24:
Jatropha podagrica

Fig. 25:
Kopsia fruiticosa

Kopsia fruiticosa

Family : *Apocynaceae*

Other names : Eng.- Pink Kopsia ; Tel- Guttigameru.

An evergreen ornamental shrub which is grown in gardens. The leaves are large. Flowers are pink which gradually fade with the advance of the day. The plant is propagated by cutting or air layering.

Fig. 25a:
Lantana camara

Lantana camara

Family : *Verbenaceae*

Native to Jamaica. A straggling aromatic shrub. Now it grows wild throughout India. The beautiful flowers come up in compact bunches. The plant is propagated by seeds or clump division.

Lawsonia alba

Family : *Lythraceae*

Other names : Eng.-Henna, Egyptian privet ; Hindi-Mehndi.

A bushy shrub of fragrant flowers. It, like the rose, needs annual pruning. The bonsai of the spherical style can be made of this species. Though cuttings strike the plant is widely propagated by seed. Pre-soaking for a few days is recommended before sowing. Seeds germinate within a week in the rains.

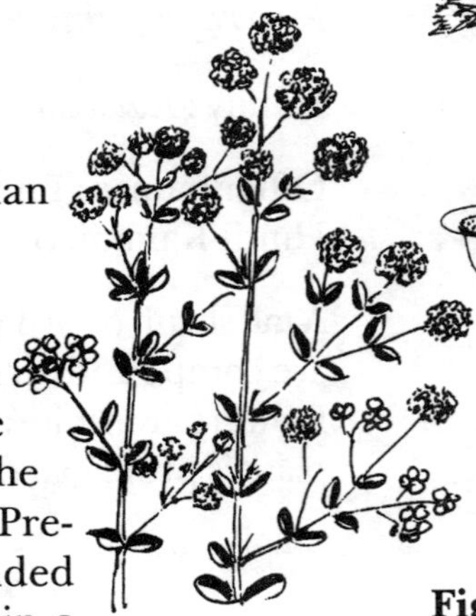

Fig. 26: *Lawsonia alba*

Malpighia coxigera

Family : *Malpighiaceae*

A small shrub of glossy leaves. It is a good ornamental grown in gardens. Its fruits are edible. The plant is propagated by cuttings.

***Rose* (Rosa *sp*)**

Family : *Rosaceae*

It is a deciduous shrub. In the temperate climate winter being the flowering season. Before the growing season the plant tends to remain dormant. Pruning of branches is essential to induce growth in the beginning of the season.

Miniature or polyantha roses are used for making a bonsai. The selected varieties should be budded on the multiflora (*Rosa multiflora*) rootstocks at a height of 30-45 cm. Then the grafts will take the shape of a miniature tree. The rose bonsai becomes an umbrella type, i.e. the trunk is straight and the head is spreading like an umbrella.

Murraya paniculata

Family : *Rutaceae*

Other names : Eng.-Orange jessamine; Hindi-Kamini, Bisar.

A tall shrub or ornamental foliage. Leaves are compound and dark green in colour. Flowers are white and sweet scented. The plant is propagated by seed or air layering.

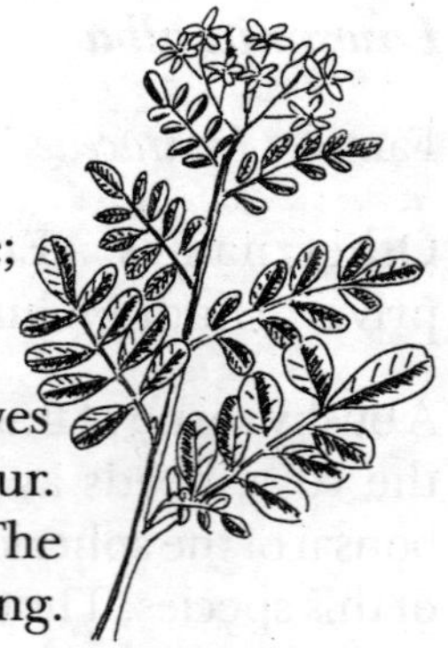

Fig. 27:
Murraya paniculata

Murraya koenigii

Family : *Rutaceae*

Other names : Eng.-Curry-leaf tree ; Hindi-Mitha-neem ; Kadhi neem.

A large evergreen shrub or small tree cultivated in south India. Leaves are used for flavouring curries. The plant is propagated by seed.

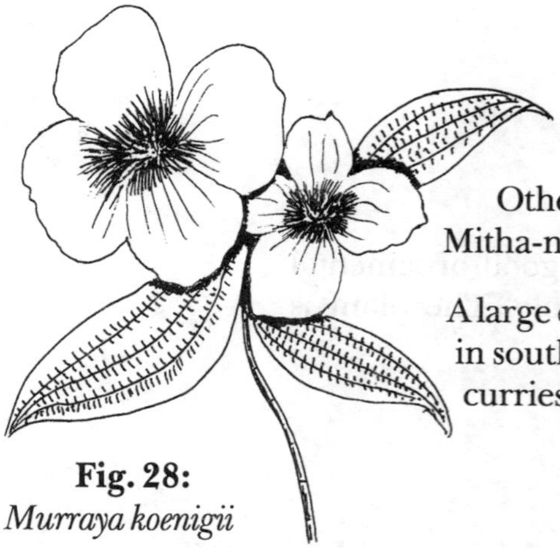

Fig. 28:
Murraya koenigii

Tibouchina semidecandra

Family : *Melastomataceae*

An ornamental shrub bearing reddish purple or violet flowers. The plant is propagated by cuttings or air layering

D

There are many trees and shrubs which are selected for flowering bonsai. Due to age the leaves of the bonsai becomes small but the size of the flowers they bear remain the same as borne by the common trees.

Albizia lebbeck

Family : *Mimosaceae*

Other names : Eng.-Lebbeck –tree; Hindi-Pili siris, Beng.-siris

A common roadside tree. It is also grown for timber and fragrant flowers. The head is spreading like an umbrella. For all these qualities it is considered to be an ideal plant for the avenues. The flat seed pods are retained even when the plant becomes leafless in winter. The plant is propagated easily by seed.

Fig. 29:
Albizia lebbeck

Bauhinia purpurea

(Already discussed in group B)

Bauhinia variegata

Family : *Caesalpiniaceae*

Other names : Eng.-Mountain ebony, Variegated Bauhinia ; Hindi- Kachnar ; Beng. - Karbur Kanchan.

A small or medium-sized tree with pink to purple fragrant flowers. Flowers appear in the leafless condition in spring. The plant is propagated by seed or cuttings. Very thick cuttings of one metre long is found to strike. A wise selection for flowering bonsai.

Fig. 30:
Bauhinia variegata

Cassia nodosa

Family : *Caesalpiniaceae*

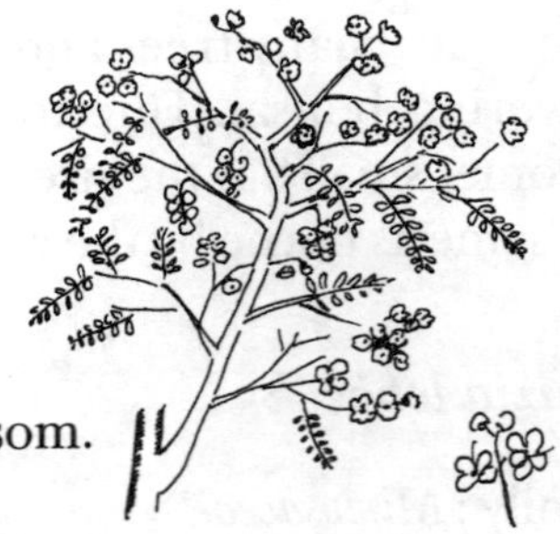

Fig. 31: *Cassia nodosa*

Native to Burma and Malaysia. The tree with short trunk and spreading head looks very ornamental. The flowers are like the apple blossom. The small bunches of pink flowers come up from the nodes of the branches. Hence the name *nodosa*. The plant is propagated from seed which should be treated with hot water before sowing.

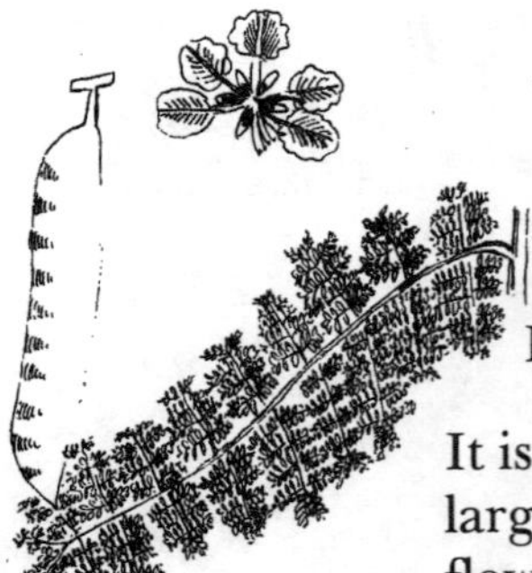

Fig. 32: *Delonix regia*

Delonix regia

Family : *Caesalpiniaceae*

Other names : Eng.-Royal Poinciana, Peacock flower ; Hindi-Gulmohor ; Beng.-Golmohor, Krishnachura.

It is a good species for flowering bonsai. The leaves are large and compound with numerous small leaflets. The flowering period is summer. The flower bunch with some leaves appear. The fruits are long and sword-like. The bonsai of Gulmohor with its symmetrical umbrella-like spreading head looks nice. It is a deciduous tree. As such all leaves fall in winter. The plant is propagated by seed.

Fig. 33: *Gardenia variegata*

Gardenia gummifera

Family : *Rubiaceae*

Other names : Eng.-Gummy cape jasmine ; Hindi-Dikamli.

A common plant of the west coast. From the growing shoot a gum of commerce (Kumbigum) is obtained. Hence the specific name *gummifera*. Flowers are white, single and fragrant. The plant is propagated by seed or air layering.

Gardenia latifolia

Family : Rubiaceae

(Already discussed in Group B)

Gardenia variegata

Family : *Rubiaceae*

It is the variegated form of *Gardenia florida*. It is an extremely floriferous variety that flowers throughout the year. Its fragrant flowers are liked by one and all. The plant is propagated by cuttings or air layering.

Holarrhena antidysenterica

Family : *Apocynaceae*

Other names : Eng.-Easter tree, Ivory tree ; Hindi- Kutaja Beng.-Kurchi.

A common flowering tree of medium height. Leaves are large. All parts of the plant bear white latex. It is propagated by seeds, suckers or etiolated cuttings obtained from the base of the plant.

Fig. 34: *Holarrhena antidysenterica*

Ixora parviflora

Family : *Rubiaceae*

Other names : Eng.-Torch tree, Small-flowered Ixora; Hindi- Jilpai, Kotagandhal.

A large shrub or small tree that bears white, fragrant flowers in compact bunches. The flush of flowers comes up in succession from April to August. The plant is easily propagated by suckers or cuttings.

Fig. 35: *Ixora parviflora*

Lawsonia alba

Already discussed in group C.

Michelia champaca

Family : *Magnoliaceae*

Other names : Eng.-Champac; Hindi- Champa

A large tree which is cultivated mainly in South India, Western Ghats, Assam and West Bengal. The plants are deciduous or semi-deciduous. It is very popular for its sweet-scented yellow flowers. The plant is propagated by seed.

Fig. 36:
Michelia champaca

Mitragyna parviflora

Family : *Rubiaceae*

Other names : Hindi-Kaddam ; Beng.-Gulikadam; Santal-Koem.

It has a great similarity with Kadam (*Anthocephalus indicus*). The leaves and flowers are comparatively small. The flowers are fragrant, which come up in abundance in spring or summer. In clay soil the plant becomes very dwarf and flowers in winter whereas in the light laterite soil the trees are tall, that flower in summer. The plant is propagated by seed or air layering.

Fig. 37:
Mitragyna parviflora

Ravenia spectabilis

Famiy : *Rutaceae*

Other name : Beng.-Laboni

A native of Cuba and Brazil. Its foliage is ornamental, lustrous and soothing to the eyes. An evergreen, medium-sized shrub. Leaves are compound and trifoliate. The flowers are attractive, which come up throughout the year, more in April-July. The plant is propagated by seed, cuttings or air layering.

E

This group is for those species the bonsai of which tend to bear fruits. Obviously it is an added attraction for which the fruit-bearing specimens are put into a special group in the show schedule. Sometimes they are not considered to be bonsai as they are grown in comparatively large pots. However a typical bonsai can bear fruits.

Fig. 38: *Annona squamosa*

Annona squamosa

Family : *Annonaceae*

Other names : Eng.-Sweet-sop, Sugar apple ; Hindi-Sitaphal, Sharifa ; Beng.-Aata

Native to south America and West Indies. A large shrub cultivated in orchard for delicious fruits. The plant is propagated by seed, cuttings or bud grafting. Sow seed in compost or cowmanure for early germination.

Fig. 39: *Archas sapota*

Archas sapota

Family : *Sapotaceae*

Other names : Eng.-Sapodilla; Hindi – Sapota, Chikku ; Beng.-Sapeta.

Native to tropical America. An overgreen tree grown widely in orchards for sweet fruits. The plant is propagated by seed or inarching. The seedlings of *khirni* (*Mimusops*

hexandra) are used as rootstocks. For bonsai the seedlings, though grow slowly, is preferable. The seedlings grow well under the shade of a tree.

Averrhoa carambola

Family : *Averrhoaceae*

Fig. 40:
Averrhoa carambola

Other names : Eng.-Carambola ; Hindi- Kamrakh; Beng.-Kamranga.

Native to Malaysia. A tree of medium height. The foliage and blossom are ornamental. It is cultivated through-out the country in the orchards. Fruits are mostly sour in taste. Carambola is used in pickle or *chatny*. A bonsai of carambola bears plenty of fruits. The plant is propagated by seed.

Carissa carandas

Family : *Apocynaceae*

Fig. 41:
Carissa carandas

Other names : Eng.-Karanda ; Hindi-Karaunda; Beng.-Karamcha.

An evergreen spiny shrub grown in gardens as a flowering ornamental, hedge plant or fruits which are pickled or used in making fruit candy (artificial cherry). The colourful fruits decorate the plant for a long time. The plant is propagated by seed or air layering.

Citrus acida

Family : *Rutaceae*

Other names : Eng.-Acid lime; Hindi- Nimbu ; Beng.-Pati lebu, Kagji lebu.

A very common spiny shrub of the home garden or Orchard. The fruits are round and juicy, used in pickle and

refreshing drinks (*Sarbat*). The plant is propagated by seed or air layering.

Citrus aurantium

Family : *Rutaceae*

Other names : Eng.-Sour orange ; Hindi-Khatta ; Beng.-Jamir.

A small tree. Fruits are used in pickle. Flowers are white, fragrant. The plant is propagated by seed or air layering. The bonsai of sour orange may bear fragrant flowers and sour fruits profusely.

Citrus aurantifolia

Family : *Rutaceae*

Other names : Eng.-Sweet lime ; Hindi-Mitha-nimbu, Beng.-Sarbati

A small tree grown in orchard for edible fruits. The fruits are completely devoid of sour taste. Hence incipid. The rind is very smooth and glossy. The plant is propagated by seed or air layering.

Citrus jambheri

Family : *Rutaceae*

Other names : Eng.-Rough orange, Hindi- Khatta ; Beng.-Jamir, Orya- Tabha.

A small tree. The fruits are strongly acid, commonly used in pickles. The seedlings are extensively used as rootstock for grafting oranges.

Citrus maxima

Family : *Rutaceae*

Other names : Eng.-Pomelo, Shaddock ; Hindi-Chakotra ; Beng.-Batabi.

A small tree cultivated in orchards for large-sized edible fruits. The plant is propagated by seed or air layering. The leaves, flowers and fruits are larger than those of any other citrus plant.

Citrus reticulata

Family : *Rutaceae*

Other names : Eng.-Mandarin, Tangerine ; Hindi-Santra.

A small tree cultivated chiefly for edible fruits. The plant is propagated by seed, air layering or bud grafting. For orchard plants mandarins are multiplied by bud grafting. The seedlings of sour orange are used as rootstocks.

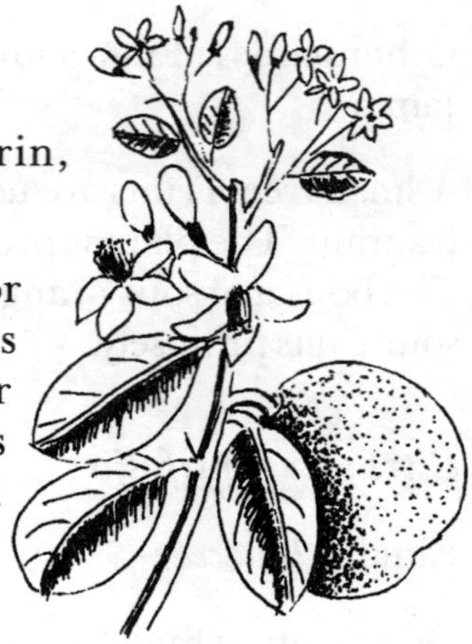

Fig. 42:
Citrus reticulata

Fig. 43:
Citrus paradisi

Citrus paradisi

Family : *Rutaceae*

Other names : Grape fruit, Beng.-Thoka batabi.

A large shrub or small tree. The fruits are smaller than pomelo. They come up in bunches. Hence the name 'grapefruit'. The plant is propagated by seed or air layering. The orchard plants are propagated by bud grafting.

Citrus sinensis

Family : *Rutaceae*

Other names : Eng.-Sweet orange ; Hindi-Musambi, Malta; Beng.-Mosambi, Sarbati.

Native to China. A small tree grown in orchards for edible fruits. The plant is propagated by seed or bud grafting. The bonsai of sweet orange may bears flowers and fruits profusely. The flower is fragrant.

Fortunella japonica

Family : *Rutaceae*

Other names : Eng.-Kumquat lime ; Beng.-Kamquat.

A small tree which bears profusely. The plants with ripe fruits are very ornamental. Fruits are small, round and the rind is glossy. It can retain ripe fruits for a few months. It is propagated by seed or air layering. The bonsai of kamquat are very ornamental with plenty of fruits.

Limonia trifolia

Family : *Rutaceae*

A bushy shrub with very small leaves, which grows well in a semi-shade condition. A very ideal species for bonsai. The ripe fruits look like the small cherry fruits. The fruits contains a sticky, scented juice and comparatively large seed. The plant is easily propagated by seed or air layering.

Fig. 44: *Limonia trifolia*

Morus indica

Family : *Moraceae*

Other name : Common mulberry ; Hindi-Tut ; Beng.-Tunt.

Native to India. Commonly found in sub-Himalayan tracts. Leaves are used to feed silkworm. The fruits are edible. The bonsai bears flowers and fruits for a long time in a year.

Psidium cattleyanum

Family : *Myrtaceae*

Other name : Eng.-Strawberry guava.

A large shrub which is native of Brazil. The leaves are small and densely set on the branches. The plant is very ornamental for its beautiful dense leaves. Fruits are very

Fig. 45: *Psidium cattleyanum*

small and edible.

Syzygium cumini

Family : *Myrtaceae*

Other names : Eng.-Java plum, Jambolana ; Hindi-Jamun; Beng.-Kalo jam.

A large tree cultivated throughout India for edible fruits. The plant is propagated by seed or air-layering.

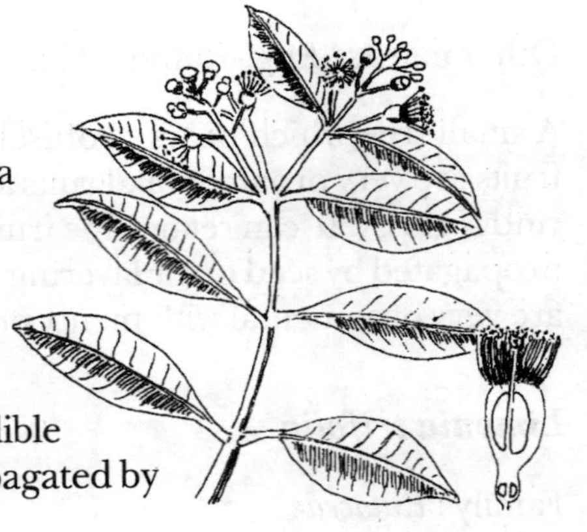

Fig. 46:
Syzygium cumini

Ziziphus mauritiana

Family : *Rhamnaceae*

Other names : Eng.-Chinese date, Jujube ; Hindi-Ber, Badara, Karkandhu, Kuvala, Pemdibar; Beng.-Kul, Badari.

Native to China. A small spiny tree. The grafted plants are cultivated in orchards. There are wild varieties that bear sour fruits. They are also edible and used in pickle. Very quick growing plants which are propagated by seed or grafting. For bonsai seed propagation is preferable.

Fig. 46a:
Ziziphus mauritiana

F

This group comprises the monocotyledonous plants such as palms, dates, cycas, etc. Monocots have no branching system. Still they, though not extensively, are used for bonsai. Monocots have no tap roots. Their roots are fibrous. Sometime their long trailing roots grow vigorously and push the soil ball out of the pot. So the root pruning once a year might be necessary. If you do not like root pruning frequently use special type of pots for the monocots (See Containers)

Palms (Family-Palmae)

The palms like *Caryota, Rhapis, Chrysalidocarpus, Livistonia, Pritchardia, Thrinax, Washingtonia* etc. are selected for bonsai. They are propagated by seed.

Dates (Family – Palmae)

The different species of the genus 'Phoenix' are grown for bonsai. Some of them are grown in orchards and others are ornamental for the gardens, still others are found in the wild, which has no economic importance. But they can be used well for making bonsai. *Phoenix roebelenii* is a dwarf ornamental palm which is ideal for bonsai.

Bamboo (Family-Gramineae)

Bamboos are the species of a number of genera. Although most of them are very tall. They are treated as shrubs. There are some very ornamental dwarf species which are grown as ornamental shrubs in the garden. There are many variegated bamboos which are also ornamental. They are *Arundinaria murieliae, Bamboosa fortunei var variegata* etc. The former is the popular yellow bamboo.

The bamboo clans grown in bonsai pots are interesting. Therefore the bonsai of bamboo has become popular.

Fig. 47: *Bamboo (Bambusa sp.)*

Cycas (Family-Cycadaceae)

The cycas is treated as a Palm.

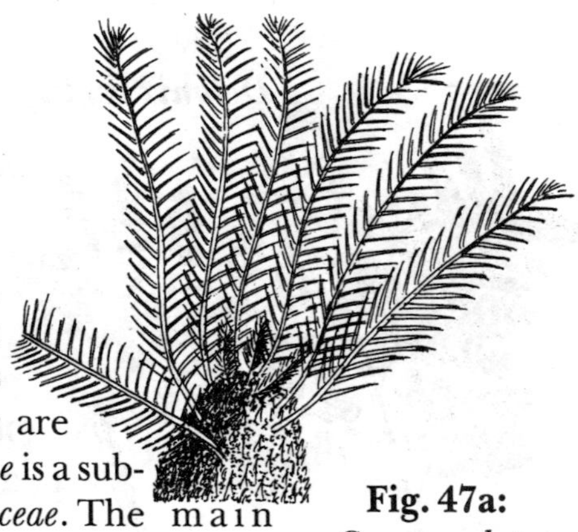

Fig. 47a: *Cycas revoluta*

G

This group of plants possess small leaves. Either simple leaves or the leaflets of a large compound leaf are small. The leaves of all species of the family *Mimosaceae* are compound with small leaflets. *Mimosaceae* is a sub-family like-*Caesalpiniaceae* and *Papilionaceae*. The main family being *Leguminoceae*. All leguminous plants have compound leaves with a number of leaflets. If the leaflets are numerous obviously they are small, e,g. 'Gulmohor', 'Copper Pod', 'Acacia' 'Sensitive plant', 'Tamarind' etc. The

leaflets are closed in the evening and spread in the morning. So the bonsai of these plants do not look so beautiful in the evening.

The species of small leaves, unlike those of large leaves, are very suitable for bonsai. On the other hand the plants bearing large leaves are considered by many not so suitable for bonsai. Because the leaf blades of a specimen of few decades many not be reduced considerably.

Acacia arabica

Family : *Mimosaceae*

Other names : Eng.-Babul Acacia, Hindi Babul; Beng.-Babla.

A medium-sized tree. Its bark exudes gum which is used in calico printing. The branches have sharp spines. The plant is propagated easily by seed.

Calliandra surinamensis

Family : *Mimosaceae*

The species of the genus *Calliandra* has very ornamental feathery leaves which are extremely dark green. The brush-like flowers are larger than other species of this genus. The plant is propagated by seed or air layering.

Delonix regia

(Already discussed in group D)

Fig. 48:
Enterolobium saman

Enterolobium saman

Family: *Mimosaceae*

Other names : Eng.-Rain tree; Monkey pod; Hindi- Vilaiti siris.

Native to America and West Indies. The plant is extensively grown in tea or coffee growing areas. In many respects it resembles *Albizia lebbeck*. The plant is propagated easily by seed.

Jacaranda mimosifolia

Family : *Bignoniaceae*

Other names : Eng.-Jacaranda ; Hindi- Nill gulmohar.

Native to brazil and N.W. Argentina. A small tree with feathery leaves and dense crown. The leaves resemble those of the family *Mimosaceae*. But it belongs to the family *Bignoniaceae*. Hence the specific name *mimosifolia* meaning the foliage is like that of the plants of the family *Mimosaceae*. The flowers are blue which come up in April-May. The plant is propagated by seed or cuttings. Air layering and bud grafting are also tried. For early flowering a seedling is budded with the scion from a floriferous tree.

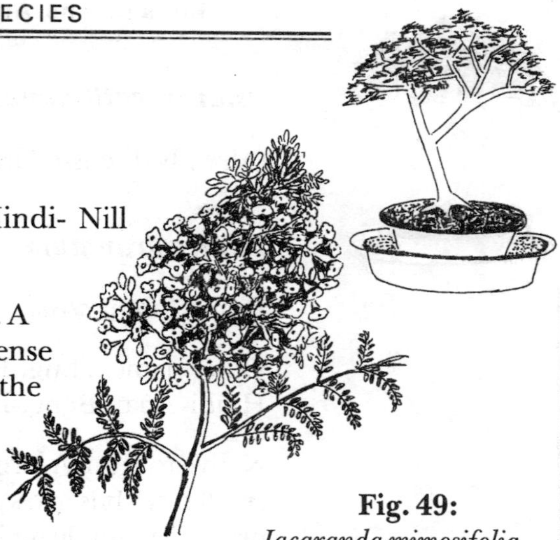

Fig. 49: *Jacaranda mimosifolia*

Phyllanthus emblica

Family : *Euphorbiaceae*

Other names : Eng.-Emblic, Indian gooseberry ; Hindi-Aonla; Beng.-Amlaki, Amla.

Native of tropical S.E.Asia. It is an orchard plant. The small fruited varieties grow abundantly in the forest. Fruits are used in pickle and fruit candy. The plant is very quick growing, which is propagated by seed or bud grafting. For making bonsai the wild varieties are preferable.

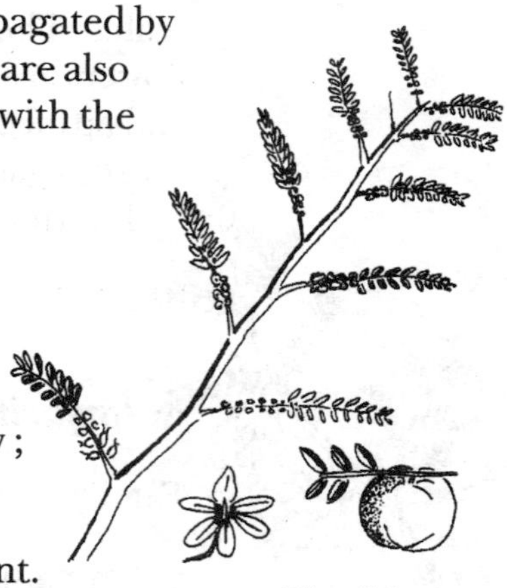

Fig. 50: *Phyllanthus emblica*

Pithecellobium dulce

Family : *Mimosaceae*

Other names : Eng.-Manila tamarind; Hindi- Vilaiti imli, Jangal jalebi

A tree of medium height. The trunk is short and the head is spreading. It is ideal for shaping a bonsai and found suitable for making a bonsai of cascade type. The plant is easily propagated by seed.

Fig. 51: *Pithecellobium dulce*

Psidium cattleyanum

(Already discussed in group E).

Punica granatum

Family : *Punicaceae*

Other names : Eng.-Pomegranate; Hindi- Anar; Beng.-Dalim, Bedana.

Native to Iran. A large shrub or small tree. It is grown as an orchard plant. Fruit juice is delicious. Seeds are also edible. The tender leaves and flowers are very ornamental and attractive. The plant is propagated by seed or air layering.

Fig. 52: *Punica granatum*

Fig. 53: *Tamarindus indica*

Tamarindus indica

Family : *Caesalpiniaceae*

Other names : Eng.- Tamarind ; Hindi-Emli; Beng.-Tentul.

Native to tropical Africa. It is grown mainly for its sour fruits which are pickled and used as seasoning spices. The plant is propagated by seed which germinates well.

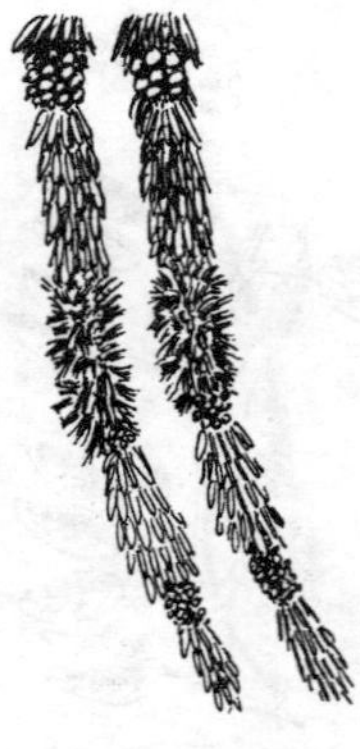

Fig. 54: *Callistemon lanceolatus.*

Callistemon lanceolatus.

Family : *Myrtaceae*

Other names : Eng.-Bottle brush ; Hindi-Lal botol brush, Beng.-Botol brush.

A large evergreen shrub or tree with drooping branches grown widely in gardens and parks as a beautiful flowering tree. The inforescence looks like a bottle brush. Hence the name (vernacular). The plant is propagated by seed or air layering.

H

This group includes the scandent or straggling shrubs. By regular pruning they are grown as an erect shrub in the gardens. So they can be used for making bonsai.

Allamanda cathartica

Family : Apocynaceae

Native to Central America and Brazil. It grows commonly as a shrub straggling over the fences or pergolas. Flowers are large and bright yellow. The plant is propagated by suckers, eliolated cuttings or ground layering.

Fig. 55: *Artabotrys odoratissimus*

Artabotrys odoratissimus

Family : *Annonaceae*

Other names : Eng.-Climbing ylang-ylang; Hindi-Harichampa ; Beng- Kanthali Champa

A large scandent shrub with greenish-yellow, fragrant flowers. The petals are fleshy. Fragrance is fruity. A buch of ber-like fruits grow from a single flower stalk. The plant is propagated by seed or layering.

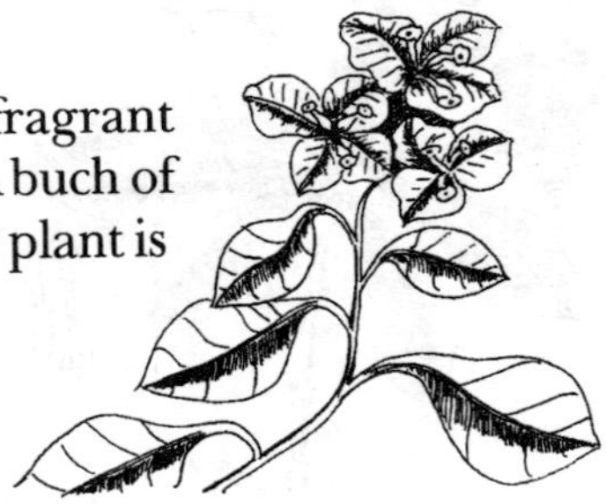

Fig. 56: *Bongain villea*

Bougainvillea

Family : *Nyetaginaceae*

A very popular garden shrub for colourful petal-like bracts. It is selected for flowering bonsai. The plant is propagated by cutting or ground layering.

Petrea volubilis

Family : *Verbenaceae*

Other names : Eng.-Purple wreath, Queen's wreath.

Native to tropical America. The plant is grown as an ornamental. It is propagated by cuttings or ground layering. It is a climbing shrub.

Fig. 57: *Petrea volubilis*

Tecomaria capensis

Family : *Bignoniaceae*

Other name : Eng.-Cape-honey-suckle.

Fig. 58: *Tecomaria capensis*

Native to South Africa. A bushy scandent shrub grown as an ornamental. The followers are orange which come up in succession in compact inflorescence : the leaves are compound and very ornamental. The plant is propagated by cutting or air layering.

I

This group comprises the evergreen shrubs and trees.

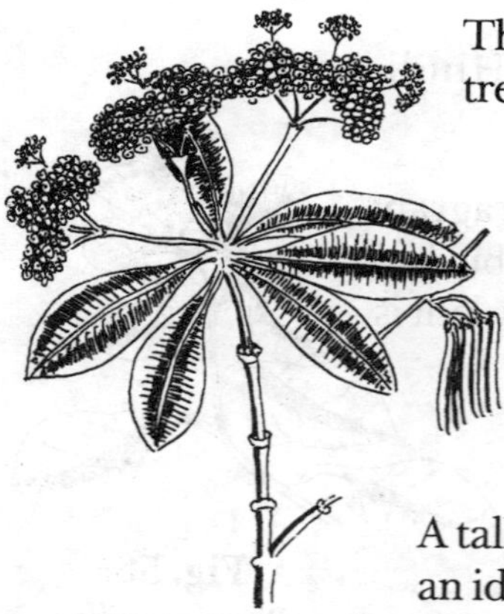

Fig. 59: *Alstonia scholaris*

Alstonia scholaris

Family : *Apocynaceae*

Other names : Eng. Devil's tree ; Hindi- Chatiun; Beng.-Chhatim, Saptaparni.

A tall evergreen tree grown along the road-sides. It is an ideal shade tree. For fragrant flowers it is also grown in parks and gardens. As a windbreak it might be grown along the western side of a large garden. The plant is propagated by seed or layering.

Araucaria cunninghamii

Family : *Araucariaceae*

Other name : Eng.-Hoop pine

Native to East Australia. It is grown as an ornamental tree. The plant is propagated from seed.

Araucaria cookii

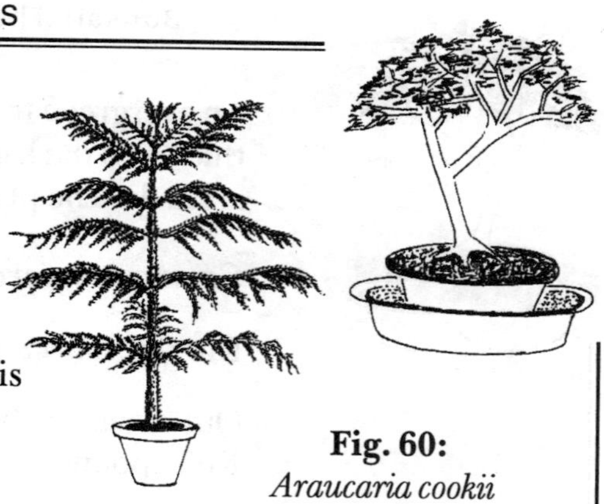

Fig. 60: *Araucaria cookii*

Family : *Araucariaceae*

Other name : Eng.-X-mass tree.

Native to East Australia. It is a very popular ornamental tree. The plant is propagated by seed.

Casuarina equisetifolia

Family : *Casuarinaceae*

Other name : Eng.-Casuarina, Sea-Oak ; Hindi- Jangli Jhau, Janglisaru.

A slender, tall evergreen tree of the East Coast. It is a common tree on the sand dune of the coastal region. It is also planted as an avenue tree. The plant is grown from seed.

Fig. 61: *Casuarina equisetifolia*

Crassula arborescens

Family : *Crassulaceae*

Native to South Africa. It is a succulent shrub. Leaves and stems are fleshy. It has a great similarity with *Portulacaria afra*. The plant is propagated by leaf cutting or stem cutting.

Cryptomeria japonica

Family : *Taxodiaceae*

Other name : Eng.-Japanese ceder, Nepal- Dhupi.

A tree of W.Himalayas, Assam, the Nilgiris and Darjeeling. The plant is propagated by seed.

Ficus retusa

Family : *Rutaceae*

Other names : Hindi and Beng.-Kamrup; Telugu-Yerakuchvi, Tam.-Kallichi, Bombay- Pilala.

An evergreen tree of ornamental foliage. Leaves are small, thick and dark green which are relished by the browsing animals. The plant is easily propagated by cuttings.

Carmona microphylla

Family : *Ehretiaceae*

Other name : Hindi and Mar. Pala ; Tam.-Kuruvingi, Oriya-Kujapponno.

A tropical evergreen tree like shrub with small, oval dark-green, shiny leaves. White flowers come up from spring to summer. It is regarded as an excellent species for bonsai. The plant is found in the forest of the laterite region. An illustration of good specimen of *Carmona* appears in Indoor Bonsai (Paul Lesniewiez).

Fig. 62: *Juniperus chinensis*

Juniperus chinensis

Family : *Cupressaceae*

Other names : Hauber, Aaraar.

A shrub or small tree, native to Europe and N. America and is distributed in W. Himalayas from Kumaon westwards. The plant is propagated by cutting air layering or ground layering.

Fig. 63: *Limonia acidissima*

Limonia acidissima

Family : *Rutaceae*

Other names : Eng.-Elephant apple, Wood apple ; Hindi-Kutbel; Beng.-Koetbell, Kotbel.

An evergreen tree bearing round sour fruits which are edible. The soft k ernel is pickled. The leaves are compound, dark green and ornamental. The plant is propagated by seed or sucker.

Mimusops elengi

Family : *Sapotaceae*

Other names : Eng.-Spanish Cherry ; Hindi-Maulsari; Beng.-Bakul.

An evergreen tree with the dense spherical head. Small whitish star-like fragrant flowers are made into garlands for hair decoration. The plant is propagated by seed. The seedlings grow well in the shade of a tree.

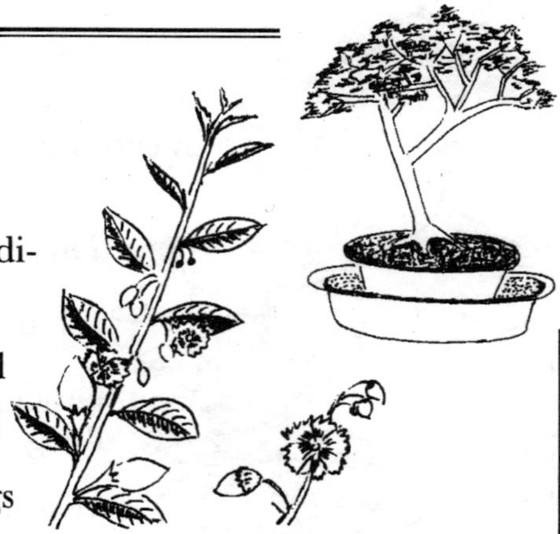

Fig. 64: *Mimusops elengi*

Mimusops hexandra

Family : *Sapotaceae*

Other names ; Eng.-Milk tree ; Hindi-Khirni, Beng.-Khirkul.

The small plants are used as the rootstock for grafting sapota. The leaves are larger than Maulsari and sapota. The stems and leaves exude white latex. The plant is propagated by seed.

Fig. 65: *Pinus longifolia*

Pinus longifolia

Family : *Pinaceae*

Other names : Long-leaved pine, Three-leaved pine ; Hindi-Chir, Salla.

Found in W. and E. Himalayas. It is very economic plant. Resin obtained from stem is used in varnishes and paints. Its leaves are long and needle-like. Hence known as 'pine needle'. The plant is propagated by seed, cutting or air layering.

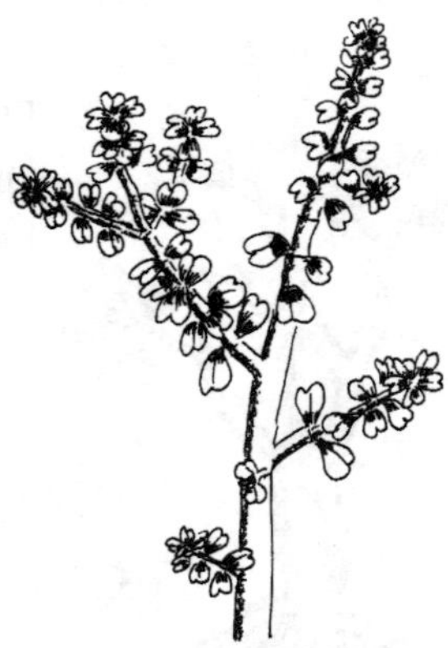

Fig. 66: *Portulacaria afra*

Portulacaria afra

Family : *Portulaceae*.

Other names : Speckboom, Elephant's food.

Native to S. Africa. It is grown in gardens. Leaves and barks

are succulent. A shrub-like evergreen which is propagated by cuttings.

Fig. 67: *Thevetia nerifolia*

Thevelia nerifolia

Family : *Apocynaceae*

Other names : Yellow oleander ; Hindi- Pilikaner ; Beng.-Kalkephul.

Native to tropical America. A shrub or small tree commonly grown in the compound of the garden as a hedge plant. Flowers are yellow, white or bronze. Leaves are long, narrow and glossy. The internodes are not conspicuous. The plant is propagated by seed which are stone-like.

Fig. 68: *Thuja orientalis compacta*

Thuja orientalis

Family : *Cupressaceae*

Other names : Eng.-Oriental Arbor-Vitae ; Hindi-Morpankhi, Mayurpankh.

A shrub or small tree with dense crown, native to China. It is grown in gardens as an popular ornamental throughout the country, and makes fine avenues in parks and gardens. The plant is propagated by seed, air layering or ground layering. Seeds need stratification for 18 months before sowing.

This group includes the plants that develop aerial roots, some of them grow thick roots that serve as the prop roots. The miniature tree having a number of prop roots or stilt roots from the horizontal branches look nice.

Fig. 69: *Ficus bengalensis*

Ficus bengalensis

Family : *Moraceae*

Other names : Eng.-Banyan ; Hindi and Beng.-Barh.

A large spreading evergreen tree extended by horizontal branches which are supported by prop roots. Leaves are

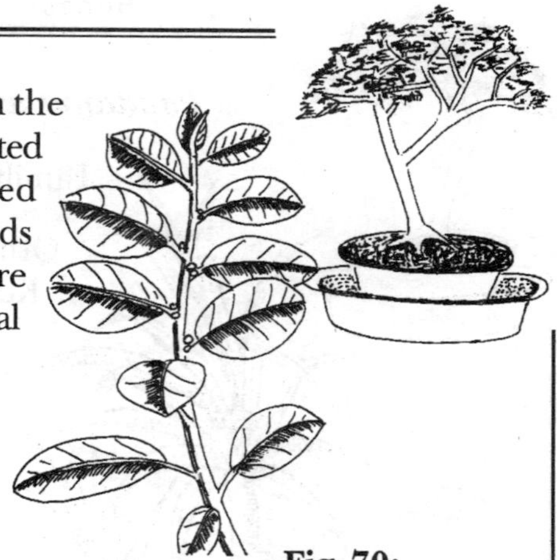

Fig. 70:
Ficus elastica

large and oval. The aerial roots arising from the branches cover the trunk. The Plant is propagated by seed, cutting or air layering (For seed propagation see Chapter 7). The air-borne seeds are deposited in the crevices of brick walls where they germinate to grow to a plant (For the special seed compost see Chapter 10).

Ficus elastica

Family : *Moraceae*

Other name : Eng.-Indian rubber tree, Assam rubber tree; Hindi-Bor ; Beng.-Raaber.

Native to India and Malaysia. A medium sized evergreen tree with thick large leaves. The stem exudes latex on bruishing. The old tree sends out aerial roots. The plant is propagated by air layering or leaf cutting.

Fig. 71:
Ficus nitida

Ficus nitida

Family : *Moraceae*

Extensively used for making bonsai. It, like *F. bengalensis*,, sends out aerial roots. The plant is propagated by cutting.

Ficus rumphi

Family : *Moraceae*

Other names : Hindi-Gagjair; Beng.-Gaiaswat, Pakur.

A small or medium sized tree. Leaves are heart shaped. Aerial roots grow from the branches. The seedlings are found to grow in the crevices on the trunk of a tree specially the date plam. The plant is propagated by seed or cuttings with aerial roots.

Fig. 72:
Ficus rumphi

Pandanus andamanensium

Family : *Pandanaceae*

Other names : Hindi – Keora, Kewda; Beng.- Ketaki, Keya.

An evergreen bushy monocot. Leaves are long with a row of sharp spine on the midrib. The leaf margins are serrated with spines. The horizontal branches are supported by the stilt roots. The plant is propagated by cuttings. The fruit, like pine apple, have seeds which are hardly used for propagation.

Fig. 73: *Pandanus andamanensium*

PLANTS FOR TRAY COMBINATION

The following plants are perennial ornamentals. Some of them have herbaceous stems. They can be chosen for tray combination.

Fig. 74: *Begonia semperflorens*

Begonia semperflorens

Family : *Begoniaceae*

A perennial herb with succulent stems. Leaves are rusty red. It flowers through all seasons. A shade-loving plant which is propagated by cuttings.

Chlorophytum comosum

Family : *Liliaceae*

A undershrub occurring in Central and Peninsular India. Leaves are linear. The flower spikes are slender that bend towards the ground. After flowering a shoot grows a number of plants which are obtained by clump division.

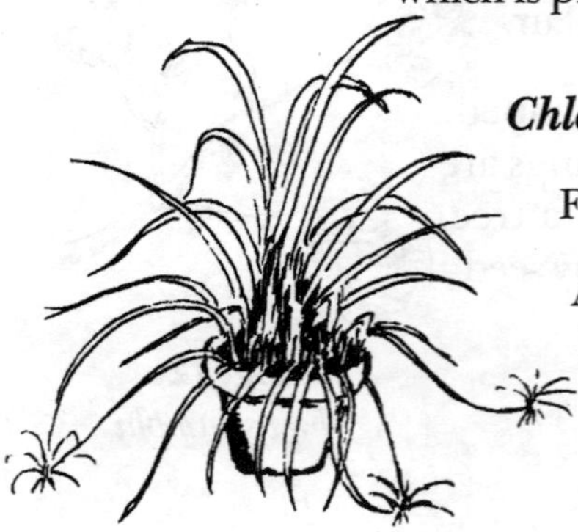

Fig. 75: *Chlorophytum comosum*

Episcia cupreata

Family : *Gesneriaceae*

Native to tropical America. A perinnial herb which is very popular for its very ornamental leaves and flowers. Leaves are hairy with serrated margins. The plant is propagated by cuttings or runners.

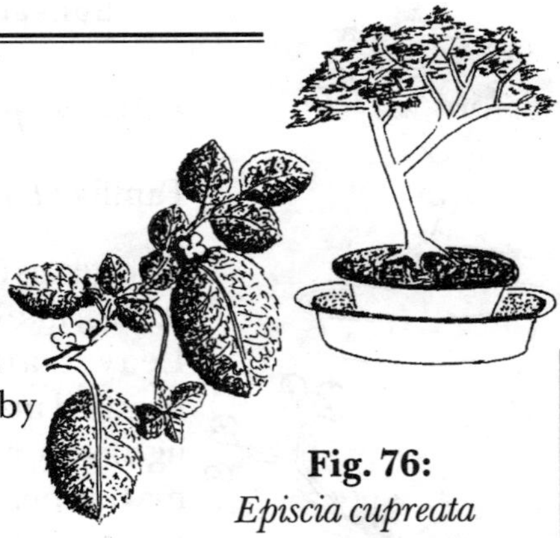

Fig. 76: *Episcia cupreata*

Strawberry (**Fragaria** *sp.)*

Family : *Rosaceae*

The plant is grown for its delicious fruits. The wild species are also available. Generally the wild species are used for this purpose. The plant is multiplied by runners.

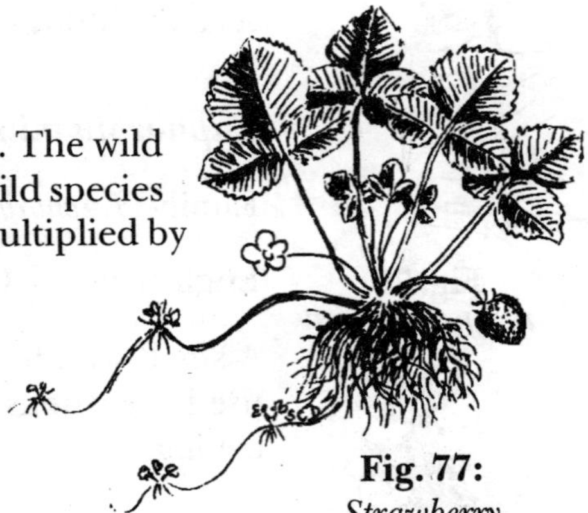

Fig. 77: *Strawberry* (*Fragaria* sp.)

Oplismenus hirtellus 'Variegatus'

Family : *Gramineae*

Ä It is an ornamental grass grown in hanging baskets. Leaves are variegated with white and pink streakes.

Sansevieria hahnii

Family : *Liliaceae*

It is commonly knows as 'Snake Plant'. This species is very dwarf. The leaves are small dark green with grey stripes (Crosswise), The plant is propagated by clump division or leaf cuttings.

Calathia ornat

Family : *Marantaceae*

In America and west Indies as many as 150 species are available. The leaves are variegated with pink stripes between the veins. The plant is propagated by clump division.

Coleus *sps*

Family : *Labiatae*

The genus *Coleus* has 150 species. The leaves, like crotons, are variegated. Leaves are heart-shaped with serrated margins. The bloches of red, light green, cream, yellow, maroon etc. may appear on the leaves. The plant is quick growing which is propagated by seed or cuttings.

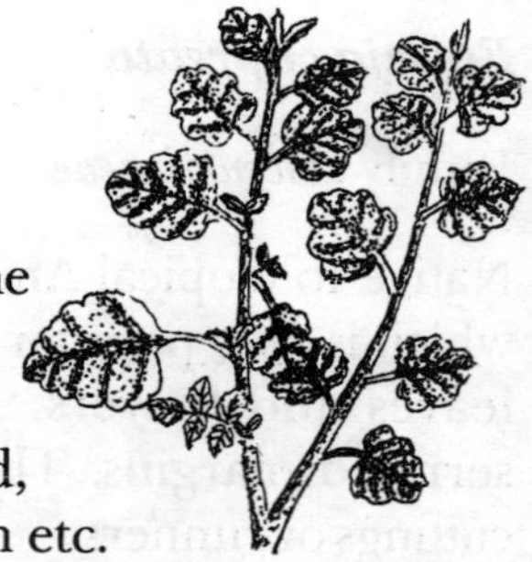

Fig. 78:
Coleus sps

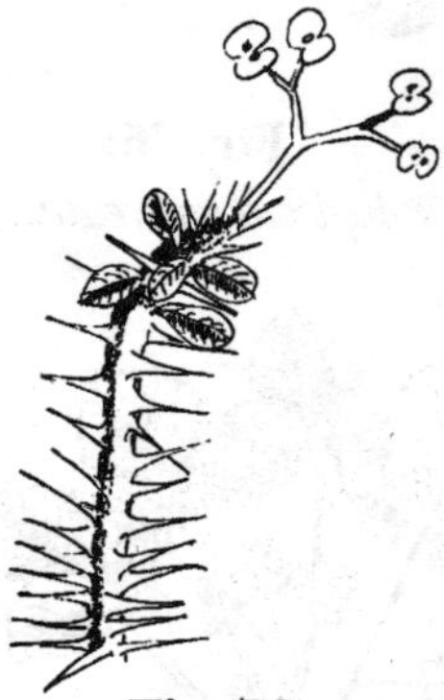

Fig. 79:
Euphorbia milii

Euphorbia milii

Family : *Euphorbiaceae*

English name : Crown of thornes.

A small scandent spiny shrub. A native to Madagasear, used in gardens for rockeries. The plant is propagated by cutting.

Fig. 80:
Impatiens balsamina

Impatiens balsamina

Family : *Balsaminaceae*

Other name : Hindi- Gul-Mehndi.

An ornamental herb grown in gardens throughout India. The stem is succulent. The plant is propagated by seed or cuttings.

Fig. 81:
Maranta leuconeura

Maranta leuconeura

Family : *Marantaceae*

The genus *Maranta* has 30 species all of which are the native of tropical America. Leaves are variegated with green and purple. The plant is propagated by cuttings.

Peperomonia argyreia

Family : *Peperomianceae*

There are more than thousand species in this genus *Peperomonia*. Very bushy and ornamental. Leaves are thick and white but veins are green. The plant is propagated by cuttings or clump division.

Fig. 82: *Peperomonia argyreia*

Portulaca grandiflora

Family : *Portulacaceae*

Other names : Eng. Rose-moss, Sunplant.

A succulent herb, native to Brazil, grown extensively as an ornamental. The plant is propagated by cuttings.

Planting Materials

For growing bonsai the planting materials are purchased from plant nurseries or grown in the gardens from seed or by vegetative methods of propagation. The most of the saplings are raised from seed or collected from their wild habitats. In this chapter both seed propagated and vegetative propagation are dealt with.

Raising seedlings

Seedlings are raised in the seed bed or seed pans. The tree seeds are mostly large but there are few which have very minute seeds, e.g. Bottle brush, Kadamba, Guli-Kadam (*Mitragyna parviflora*) etc. Raising seedlings from the minute seeds is very difficult.

When the quantity of seed is small a seed pan is used for sowing. The shallow pots of burnt clay having 30cm. in diameter and 7 cm. depth are generally used as seed pans. On crocking the pots are filled with seed compost. The word crocking is used to mean the act of placing a pot shred with its concave side downwarsds over the drain hole of the pot. For the drainage of surplus water crocking is a must. A layer of 2-3cm. thickness of aggregate is laid on the crock. The aggregate should be a mixture of grit and coarse sand. Grit is obtained by sieving coarse sand. A mixture of stone chips of very small size, say 3-5mm. cubes and coarse sand may also be used instead. After this operation the pot is filled with the seed compost. The surface level of the compost should remain just below the rim. The empty space is necessary for holding water while watering. The following is the seed compost that can be used in the seed pans.

Medium loam	One bucket (10 litre cap.)
Humus (Leafmould/cowmanure)	2 litre.
Super phosphate	50 g.
Muriate of Potash/Wood ash	50 g.
Magnesium sulphate	20 g.
Chalk dust ($CaCO_3$)	15 g.

Keep the compost in a moist condition for a week, then fill the seed pans with this compost and then sow the seeds as usual, i.e. they should be distributed evenly over the entrire surface. Then cover the seeds by sprinkling fine-grained cowmanure or sand. The cover should not be thicker than the thickness of the seed laid over the compost. Then water the pan thoroughly with a water can fitted with its fine rose. On watering if the seeds are exposed at places then cover them again as before. Care should be taken to see that the cow manure to be used for covering the seeds must be moist. Seeds before germination hardly need light, direct or diffused. To keep them in the dark cover the pan with a piece of hessian. Do not use polythin sheet for this purpose in hot weathers. The hessian if used should be kept soaked in water. Watering once a day is the usual practice. As soon as the germinated seed raise their head the cover (hessian) must be removed.

Seeds should not be sown thickly. Because the congested seedlings fall victim to the damping off disease. By this disease the portion of the seedlings just above the soil level rots. On incidence the unaffected seedlings should be removed and transplanted in a new pot thinly. Before pricking out spray the seed pan with a copper fungicide like Blue copper, Fytolan or Blitox thoroughly.

How to Sow the fine seed

Seeds of Bottle brush, Kadamba, Guli Kadamba etc. are minute. On sowing the seed should not be covered with manure or sand. First, fill the seed pan with potting compost and sterilize it with the formalin solution. Obviously the potting compost must be fine-grained.

1. Before sowing soak the potting compost with water by using the fine rose of a water can.

2. Seed should be sown evenly. For the convenience of sowing the fine seeds should be mixed with fine sand or wood ash at the ratio of 1:4.

3. On sowing watering should be done by a sprayer ;

4. To keep the compost moist for a day or so cover the seed pan with a glass pane.

5. Water the seed-pan as needed by a sprayer.

6. On germination cover the germinated seed with a thin layer of cow manure. This is to be done by a fine sieve. Hold the sieve with a little of fine-grained cow manure and move gently over the pan. The thickness should be just to cover the germinated seeds. After two days the process may be repeated if necessary.

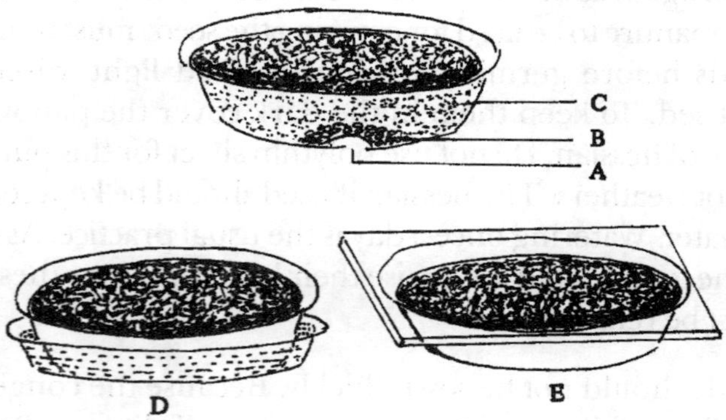

Fig. 83: *Seed-pans*

A- Drain hole
B- Aggregates
C- Potting compost
D- Watering by capillary method
E- Cover of glas pane

7. To prevent quick drying the soil of the seed-pan should be soaked from below. The capillary system of watering is more scientific. The seed pan can be soaked by the process as oil rises through the wick of a lamp. The process is known as the capillary rise of a liquid. Thus water from the shallow water table of the earth rises to the surface.

Put the seed pan in a shallow pot containing water. The water of the pot will rise slowly through the drain hole of the pot and soak the soil completely. Fill the pot with water when watering is needed. Instead of a seed-pan a brick can be used. Place a brick on a shallow pot. Put a layer of potting compost over the brick which will serve as a seed bed. Sow the seed as usual.

Fill the pot with water which will rise through the brick and soak the soil layer. When watering will be needed fill the pot with water.

Vegetative Propagation

The vegetative parts like shoots, roots, leaf buds suckers etc. are used in propagating many garden plants.

Cuttings: Most of the ornamentals, fruits and few vegetables are propagated by shoot cuttings. The cuttings are of two types – soft wood and hard wood. For some plants soft cuttings from the top of the shoots strike well, e.g. hibiscus, gardenia etc. The one year-old hard-wood cuttings of hibiscus, gardenia tabernaemontana, cerbera, plumeria, tecomeria, bougainvillea root well. The rose, mulberry, grape, custard apple etc. are propagated by hard wood cuttings.

Fig. 84: Cuttings

A- Hard cutting
B- Soft cutting

The size of the soft-wood cuttings should be small, i.e. 7-12 cm. long. The length of a hard wood cutting varies from 15-30 cm. The soft wood cuttings should retain few leaves whereas the hard cuttings should be made leafless. The cuttings may be treated with root hormone powder for early rooting. The application of hormone powder not only increases the rate of success but also helps to erupt more roots. This becomes helpful to establish the plant early. The hard cuttings taken in winter should be exposed to the direct sun. On the contrary the soft cuttings should be placed in shade in a humid surrounding so that the cuttings do not wilt. To apply hormone powder dip the base of the cuttings in water and shake off extra water by jerking, then insert the base one centimeter deep in the hormone powder strike the cutting on the rim of the container. After 10 minutes of this operation insert the base of the cuttings in the rooting medium which should be sand or sandy loam. The cuttings strike within 3-6 weeks. But the soft cuttings root early, i.e. within 6-15 days.

Root cuttings: Many dicots send out suckers. They can be propagated by root cuttings. The light and laterite soil is very favourable for the sucker growth. For this reason in the heavy soil suckering is less. The root cuttings of guava, bael, wood apple, millingtonia etc. can be used for propagation. The 20cm. long cuttings should be taken. They should be inserted into the soil upto 16cm. leaving only 3-4 cm. above the soil level. Within a few weeks the leaf bud will grow to become a shoot.

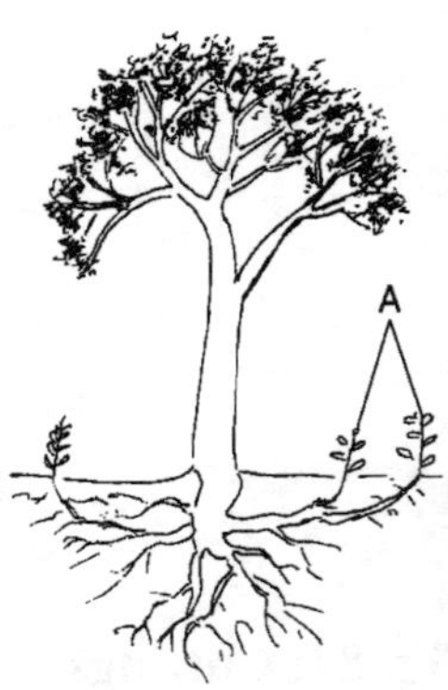

Fig. 85: Suckers (A)

Suckers: In light or laterite soils many ornamentals and fruit plants sprout suckers. Guava, bael, wood apple, passion flower, lemon, aonla, ixora, millingtonia send out plenty of suckers. Monocots like pine apple, ginger lily, canna, ornamental bamboo etc. go on producing suckers. To grow them into independent plants the suckers should be detached from the mother plant and planted as rooted cuttings in 12cm. pots. After few months' growth they can be planted as saplings.

Runners: The runner are the shoots that grow like branches touching the soil surface. The adventitious roots develop from the nodes or leaf joints of the runners. Strawberry, *Pudina*, sambac (*Jasminum sambac*) etc. grow runners. For the purpose of multiplication a runner can be divided into pieces each having a node with its root growth. Then they are planted like the rooted cuttings.

Ground layering: The ornamental shrubs of cane-like stems are very suitable for this type of propagation. Nerium, allamanda, bougainvillea etc. are multiplied by this method.

This flexible stems are bent to touch the ground. With a sharp knife, a notch is made on the stem by two slanting cuts closely but in the different planes. It will be better if a tongue is made by cutting slantwise. The tongue should be

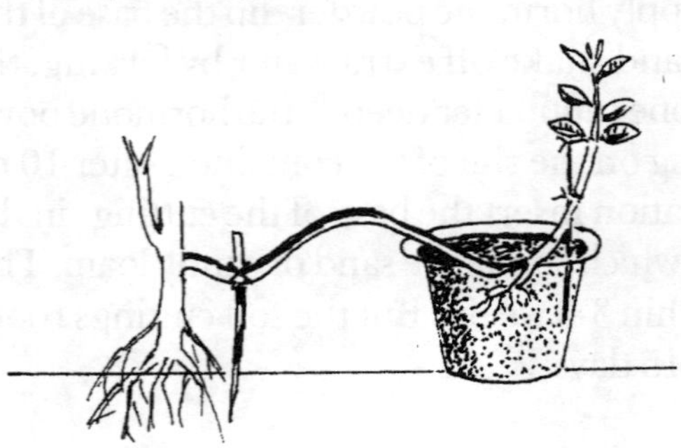

Fig. 86: Ground layering

on the side of the shoot. To open the tongue a matchstic is inserted into the cut as shown in the figure.

A shallow hole is dug to put the layer below the ground level. The layer is covered with the sufficient quantity of soil that will be kept moist for 6-8 weeks within which the tongue will develop roots. To detach the layer from the mother plant the stem is cut 10cm. away from the tongue in 2-3 steps. This will help stand the shock of detachment. The rooted layer is lifted carefully from the ground and planted in the pot as is done in case of rooted cuttings. This type of layering can be done in pots instead of the ground.

Air layering: It is also known as marcottage or *Gootikalam* or *Gooti*. A shoot of about 30-45 cm. long is selected for air layering. A griddle is made at a point of 30-40cm. from the tip by removing the ring of bark of 15-20mm. wide. While removing the bark care should be taken to expose the wood completely. Then scrape the silvery portion of the exposed wood to prevent healing. To hasten rooting apply root hormone powder on the cut of the bark where roots will erupt. About 100 grams of moist sphagnum moss is placed round the stem to enclose the cut surface. Hold the moss ball in position and get it wrapped up with a piece of alkathene film (150mm x 90mm). The two ends must be twisted and tied with a piece of jute twine(*sutli*) so that water cannot steep inside. Another technique is to use both soil and sphagnum moss. First, the griddle is covered with a soil ball which is then covered with moist moss. To wrap the moss the polythene film is not so necessary.

Fig. 87: Air layering

If layering is tried in the humid period of the year 2-6 week time is generally needed for rooting. The growing roots can be seen through the alkathene film. Detach the layer from the mother plant when the shoot has resumed growth. On detaching remove the alkathene film and transplant the layer in a pot. Then place the pot in a shady corner until the roots take soil.

Mound layering: It is also known as 'stool layering'. The shrubs producing a good number of stems from the ground level can be propagated by mound layering. Nerium, allamanda hibiscus, ixora, cestrum, jasmine etc. can be propagated by mound layering. If a tree is cut leaving a short stump on the ground a good number of shoots will grow from the base. Those shoots can be used for mound layering. This method is followed in the old guava orchard when its productivity is lowered. Just before the setting in of the monsoon a mound of earth is made covering the base of the plants. The stems within the mound will develop roots within a few months. On removing the mound the rooted stems/ branches are detached and planted as rooted cuttings. If mound layering is tried in spring or summer watering should be done regularly to soak the mound.

Clump division: The shrubs or herbaceous perennials that grow new rooted offshoots in abundance are multiplied by the method of crown division. Allamanda, jasmine, nerium, lantana etc. can be propagated by clump division.

Fig. 88: Clump division

GRAFTING

In grafting two different species of the same genus are required. In general a delicate species or cultivar does not develop any strong root system from its vegetative parts. Therefore cutting, layering etc. are not found suitable for those plants. As their seeds do not breed true to their mother type grafting is the only answer. Because in grafting the shoots (scion) of a mother plant are grafted onto the stocks having stronger roots, which must be a closely related species. For example, for grafting the rose of a garden variety a wild rose is required as a rootstock.

Approach grafting: It is the oldest method of grafting which is also known as 'Inarching'. Before the introduction of bud grafting the inarching was the only method of grafting. In this process the rootstock is brought very close to the mother plant. A suitable branch for use as a scion should be selected. Its thickness must be the same as that of the rootstock. One year old branches of the pencil thickness are suitable for this type of grafting. In approach grafting both the stock and the scion grow independently on their own roots. To bring about the union at the point of contact a slice of wood (4-6cm long) half of the thickness from each of the stock and the scion is removed carefully with a sharp knife. The point of union should be tied tightly with a suitable cord. On healing the joint of the cut surfaces the graft is separated from the mother plant. In this operation the top of the stock and the base of the scion are gradually severed. On separation the graft should be provided with a stake and be kept in a partially shady place for a week or so.

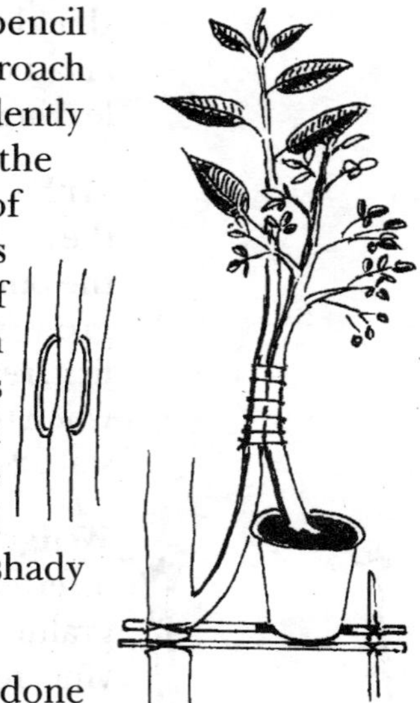

Fig. 89: Approach grafting (Inarching)

Bud grafting : It is a kind of grafting which is done conveniently by keeping the mother plant and the stock at a distance from each other. A rootstock of a closely related species is selected, i.e. the stock and the scion plant must belong to the same family.

The common type of budding is know as 'T'-budding or 'shield budding'. A cross cut (2-4cm) is made on the stem of the rootstock deep enough just to cut the bark (2-4cm) a few centimetre above the ground level. Then starting about 2 cm. below make a vertical cut to meet the first cut to form a 'T'. To loosen the bark give the knife a slight twist on either side for making room for the bud. Collect a scion with the 'eyes' from the shoot of a few week old. The term 'eye' is used to mean the bud of a leaf joint. Trim the leaf stalks one centimeter above the joints. Then

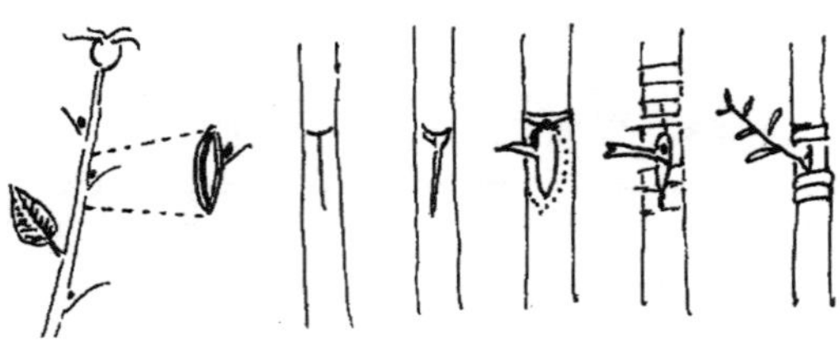

Fig. 90: Bud grafting

remove the thorns, if any, by snapping them off. With the sharp end of a budding knife lift the bud with a slice of wood of the scion. The wood portion under the 'eye' should be removed carefully without bruishing the shield. The trimmed leaf stalk which is one centimeter long will serve as the handle or the shield. Holding the handle insert the shield in the 'T' shaped cut and tie it carefully with an alkathene strip strarting from below and working upwords leaving the 'eye' itself uncovered.

Within 2-3 weeks the bud will swell as a sign of growth after the bud union has taken place. Remove all the shoots below the bud and trim the head of the stalk to force the bud to grow. The trimming should be done in two steps. In the first, remove only the twigs. In the second and the final stage when the bud grows to a shoot of 3-4 cm. long cut back the stalk 2-3cm. above the bud joint.

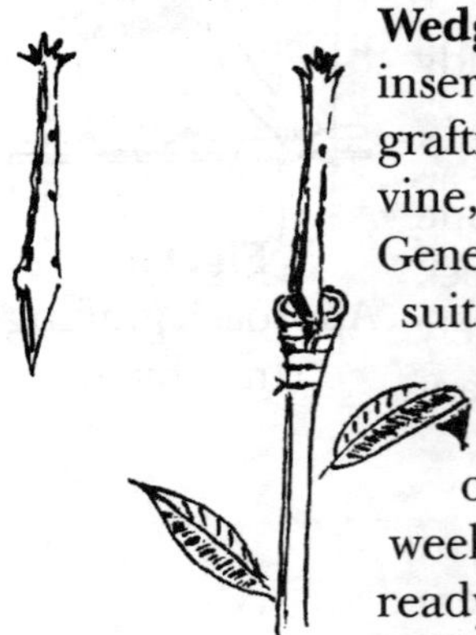

Fig. 91: Wedge grafting

Wedge grafting: In this process of grafting a scion shoot is inserted into the cleft made at the top of the rootstock. For grafting mango, hibiscus, *Champa* (*Michelia*), Camelia, grape vine, magnolia etc. wedge grafting is considered suitable. Generally one-year-old seedlings are grown for grafting. The suitable period for grafting is June to September. The rootstock is decapitated and a cleft is made at the top to receive the scion. To force the scion cut the leaves of 10-12 cm. long shoots leaving the leaf stalks. After a week when the stalks (petioles) will drop the scion becomes ready for grafting. Two long slanting cuts (15cm long) are made with a sharp knife on the both sides of the basal end. It is very necessary that the end of the wedge comes to a point. It should be very smooth, which is made by a single cut on each side with a very sharp knife. The wedge of the scion is inserted into the cleft of the stock. The graft joint is tied with a strip of polythene film so that rain water cannot get into it. After a week or so the scion will begin to grow.

Bonsai Nursery

Due to the growing popularity of bonsai the demand in the market has been created. Those who cannot afford time and patience for growing bonsai stoop to procure it from the nursery. Therefore many nurserymen have developed a section of bonsai with a view to supplying not only the bonsai but also the plant materials which are specially needed for making bonsai. Three to five year old plant trained for a bonsai take a shape favourable for a bonsai. The cost of such plants are much cheaper than a specimen bonsai. Obviously the nurseries select the species which within a few years of growth become a young bonsai. A rooted cutting of pencil thickness of guggul (*Commiphora mukul*) has become a bonsai in only three years of growth. No pruning or training was adopted. It has been illustrated in this book. The following species might be selected by the bonsai nurseries for making young or semi-bonsai within a few years.

Guggul (*Commiphora mukul*)

Plumeria sps
Karambola
Ficus bengalensis
Ficus retusa

Mulberry (*Morus nigra*)
Tamarindus indica

Kamquat
(*Fortunella japonica*)
Citrus trifolia
Gardenia florida 'Variegata'
Bauhinia variegata
Bougainvillea
(cv. Partha, Subhra etc.)
Jasminum multiforum
Jasminium auriculatum.

The bonsai of *Ficus bengalensis* is highly liked by many. Because the miniature tree having a number of prop roots is very attractive. But the grower cannot have the sufficient number of seedlings. The seedlings grow from the air-borne seeds deposited in the crevices of the walls. To have a good number of seedlings the seeds of a banyan tree are sown in the seed compost of old mortar which can be collected from the dilapited buildings. A suitable seed compost for sowing banyan seeds has been discussed in Chapter – "POTTING COMPOST."

Fig. 92: *Plumeria acutifolia*

A list of nurseries dealing in bonsai or the planting materials for making bonsai has been appended in the last.

Containers for Bonsai

The term BONSAI in the Japanese itself indicates the form of the container. It should be plate-like, i.e. very shallow. Both the aspects of beauty and utility are considered in designing the pots for bonsai. The shape of the pot should be harmonious with the form of a miniature tree. Through training the trunk line is brought to the desired shapes to imitate the forms we find in nature. It is, however, imperative to bring about harmony between the trunk-line and the shape of the pot. If it is achieved the beauty of the miniature tree will be enhanced. The width and the depth should correspond to the volume of soil necessary for the particular specimen. In otherwords the quantity of soil required for the mini, medium and large bonsai must differ. Accordingly the size and shape of the pots should necessarily be different. The colour of the pots should not contrast diagonally with the foliage, flowers and fruits. In other words, the colour harmony should be there.

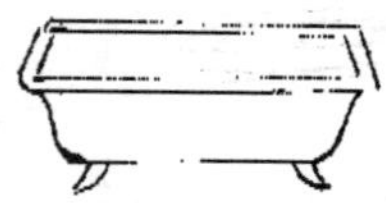

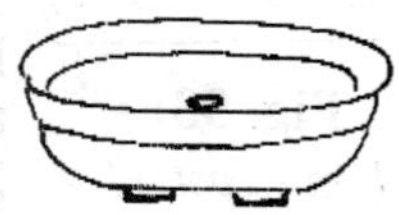

The shapes of bonsai pots are many e.g. square rectangular, oval, circular, hexagonal, octagonal etc. The bonsai experts of Japan and USA have recommended the specification of pot shapes to suit the particular trunk style. According to them, the upright style looks elegant in square or rectangular pots. The oval pots are suitable for the informal upright or curved trunks. The cascade bonsai needs a deep pot to balance the one-sided growth of the tree. The depth of a pot for the semi-cascade should obviously be less than that for a full cascade. The trunk of serpentine curves suits better in long and shallow pots. The styles of double trunk, multitrunk, raft etc. look better in long pots.

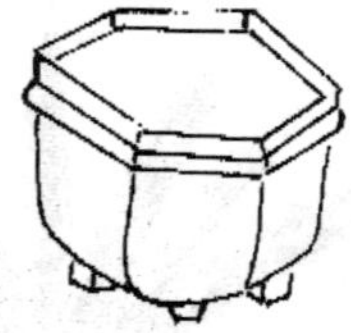

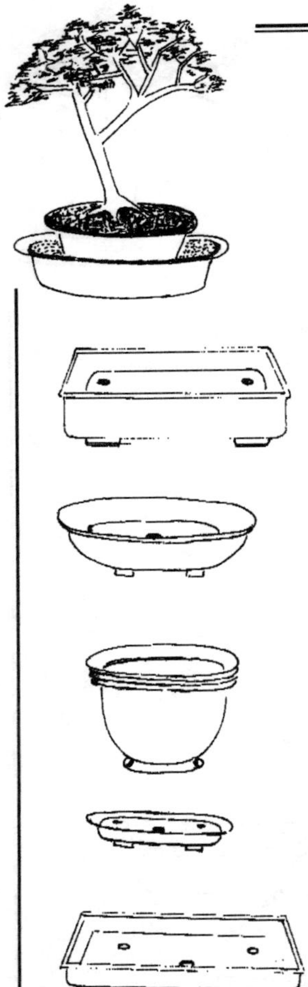

Fig. 93: *Bonsai pots of different shapes and sizes*

The long pots may be rectangular or oval, the width of which will be half of the length. The blocks of stone, bricks are used for growing bonsai. They are however placed in a plate-like container which has to hold a little water while watering.

Many growers like to have a pot with bright colour and ornamental carvings. The ornamental shapes are desirable but attractive colours or curvings will distract the attention from the main object. The pots of burnt clay are mostly used for bonsai. They are either brick red or terracotta colour. The later is preferable to the former. The pots should not be coloured with the paint containing oil. Because it seals the pores of the pot wall. The pores of the pot walls are helpful for aeration in the pot soil. The growing roots get oxygen through the pores of the pot. For this reason the roots are found to crowd forming a mat along the sides of the porous pots. The roots need oxygen for respiration that supplies them energy for growth and activity. The pots of cement concrete, porcelain, plastic, fibre glass or clay pots with painted surface cannot supply oxygen to the roots through the pot walls. But the painting clay pots with a distemper of red oxide, quick lime (CaO) and water is admissible. With this paint the discoloured pot surface brightens as new pots. The mixture of lime and red oxide (1:2) gives the brick-red colour which is pleasing. And this distemper does not close the pores. Hence preferable. Nevertheless the pots of various colours are marketed and used widely by the bonsai growers that might be a novice or expert. In that case the selection of colours should be wise because the colour of the pot must not contrast sharply to the living object. The mild contrast which is used to bring about the colour harmony should be followed here. For example, evergreen bonsai with dark-green foliage will be in harmony with the pots of reddish brown, grey or green colour. On the contrary the light green foliage and white or grey trunk will be in conformity with the lighter colour of the pot. The dimension of the pot should be proportionate. The length and breadth should not be much larger than the spread of the branches. This rule, however, holds good in case of the tree having straight trunk with short drooping branches. The length of the pot of a single tree should not exceed two-thirds the height of the tree. In case of the group

Fig. 93a: *Monocot in a narrow-mouthed pot*

planting the pot length should nearly be the same as two thirds the height of the tallest tree of the group. The depth of the pot should normally be in conformity with the thickness of the trunk. It should be upto 2.5 times the base of the trunk. For an old tree with very thick stem the pot depth should be the same as the base of the trunk. In case of the cascade style the depth of the pot should be half of the trailing stem.

Potting Compost

Soil (Clay or loam), humus (organic residues) and fertilizers (organic or chemical) are mixed proportionately to prepare a potting compost to plant saplings for bonsai. Potting compost used for growing pot plants can be primarily used for bonsai. Generally nitrogen-rich compost should not be used. Nitrogen is supplied to plants from two different sources which are organic or chemical. Chemical nitrogen is not recommended for bonsai. Because it makes the plant quick growing that produces long internodes. Obviously it is considered not feasible to the dwarfing process. Even the organic substances containing more nitrogen should not be used liberally. They are oilcake, hoof and hornmeal, fish meal, bloodmeal, leather meal etc. On the contrary leafmould, compost, cow manure etc. contain less nitrogen. They can be used safely. Generally they are regarded as the soil amendments. Because they add humus to the soil, that improves the soil structure. Humus not only improves soil structure but also retains moisture. Any soil devoid of humus cannot be used for agricultural purposes. The term 'soil' in agriculture means the soil that contains humus Roots, leaves herbaceous stems, flowers, fruits, seeds etc. form humus on decomposition. The quantity of humus as needed by the different crop of flowers, fruits and vegetables is not the same. So for a particular crop humus has to be added to the soil accordingly.

Humus-rich soil should be used in preparing the potting compost for bonsai. Because humus will improve the structure of the compost which will facilitate the drainage of excess water and soil aeration. Soil and humus are the

main ingredients of the potting compost. Soil itself consists of three ingredients, e.g. clay, silt and sand. The soil character is changed with the variation of the quantity of the ingredients present. Accordingly the different soil samples are termed as clayey, loamy or sandy. However the conditions indicated by the above terms are however related to soil texture. The textural value of the soil varies with the quantity or the ingredients present. As such the terms 'fine', 'course' and 'medium' are used to indicate the textural value of a particular soil sample. The fine-textured soil is heavy. Because it contains mainly the clay particles which are very fine. The pore spaces between the clay particles are minimum. So such soil suffers from the bad drainage and bad aeration. The soil becomes compact and the rootlets hardly get oxygen for respiration. On the contrary the coarse-textured soil contains mainly the sand particles, which are much larger than the clay particles. Hence the coarseness. Silt is a quartzic substance. Its particles are also fine which cannot be separated from the clay particles easily. If a soil contains clay and sand in a ratio of 1:1 is known as 'loam'. Heavy loam contains more clay and less sand, nearly in a ratio of 2:1. On the contrary the light loam contains two parts of sand and one part of clay.

Clayey soil is heavy and sticky. The structural value of such soil is very poor. To improve its structure add humus in the form of leafmould, compost or cow manure. The soil with the granular structure is very suitable for growing garden plants, so also bonsai. To effect good drainage and aeration well-structured soil is necessary. A loam with 50 per cent of clay and 50 per cent of sand is called medium-textured soil. A heavy or fine-textured soil is not so suitable for most garden plants. To change the textural value of a fine-textured soil sand has to be mixed with it. On the contrary clay has to be mixed with the sandy soil proportionately to have the desired textured.

Besides humus fertilizer mixture with balanced N.P.K. is needed to add sufficient plant nutrients that will help sustain growth. All the ingredients of the potting compost are divided into three types, e.g. Soil, humus and fertilizer mixture. Although soil and humus can supply certain amount of plant nutrients, they are not considered enough for proper growth and development. Of course a virgin soil is rich in plant food. The top soil under the forest vegetation is rich in humus. So what it needs is only the fertilizer mixture. Besides all these a soil needs lime (Calcium carbonate, ($CaCO_3$) to attain the desired pH value. If the soil is not too acid lime should not be used. The pH range from 6-7 is suitable for most crops. For most bonsai (species) pH 6.5 is suitable. Lime-loving species are very few, which are grown for bonsai. Even camellia which prefers alkaline soil in the ground thrives well in acid soil in pots. If pH is below 6 10-20 grams of pulverized chalk should be mixed with a bucket (10 litre capacity) of soil.

The fertilizer mixture should not contain chemical nitrogen. Organic nitrogen can be used instead. Hoof and hornmeal, oil cake etc. are commonly used as nitrogenous manure. Fishmeal, bloodmeal, leathermeal, poultry manure are also rich in nitrogen, but they are hardly used in the potting compost. Cowmanure and leafmould also contain nitrogen but in a very little quantity.

For bonsai the potting compost must be rich in phosphate and potash. Bonsai needs plenty of phosphorous for its stronger growth. Nitrogen makes the growth soft and shappy, but phosphorous makes it hard and strong. The strong growth can resist the deadly disease like dieback. Phosphorous makes the roots stronger which become capable of absorbing more nutrients. The main sources of phosphorous are bonemeal and superphosphate, the former being organic and the later chemical.

The rapid growth made by nitrogen is due to the rapid multiplication of cells. These cells must be filled up with carbohydrates and other synthesized products. The role of potash is to build up these products. Potassium, like phosphorous causes early maturity and makes the wood of the bonsai hard and strong, essential for resisting dieback and many other diseases. In summer when much loss of water takes place by transpiration through leaf pores (stoma) potash saves the plants by inhibiting the process of transpiration. The chief sources of potash are very few. They are wood ash, sulphate of potash and muriate of potash and nitrate of potash (*Sora*). It is obvious that wood ash is

the organic source and the other are inorgaganic or chemical.

In the potting compost a different kind of substance is used for the better growth of the tree. It is mortar that can be collected from the dilapidated old building. The mortar is a substance which is a mixture of sand, *surki* and lime, which is used as lime concrete or bonding material in masonry works. If old mortar is not available only a few-month-old mortar can be used. Mix pulverized brick or burnt clay, sand and lime (CaO) in the ratio of 10:5:1. Soak the mixture with water and leave it for a few months for seasoning. Crumble the staff before use in the compost. This mortar if mixed with a little humus (leafmould) can be used as a seed compost for sowing the seeds of *Ficus bengalensis* and *Ficus religiosus*.

Any of the following potting compost can be used for bonsai

1

Heavy loam	...	1 bucket (10 litre capacity)
Compost/leafmould	...	3 L
Oil cake (pulverised)	...	150g
Bonemeal	...	200g
Mortar(old/seasoned)	...	500g
Wood ash	...	100g
Magnesium sulphate (Mag. sulf.)	...	25g

2

Loam (medium)	...	10 litre
Cowmanure	...	3 litre
Leafmould	...	2 litre
Hoof and hornmeal	...	300g
Super phosphate	...	200g
Muriate of potash	...	100g
Magnesium sulphate (Mag. sulf.)	...	500g

3

Clay (heavy soil)	...	10 litre
Cowmanure/compost	...	4 L
Leafmould	...	1 L
Hoof and hornmeal	...	300g
Super phosphate	...	200g
Muriate of potash	...	100g
Mag. sulf.	...	25g
Mortar	...	500g.

4

Light loam	...	10 litre
Clay	...	2 L
Cowmanure/compost	...	3 L
Leafmould	...	1 L
Mortar	...	400 g
Bonemeal	...	200 g
Woodash/Muriate of potash	...	100g
Mag. sulf.	...	25 g.

5

Clay (Heavy soil)	...	10 litre
Sand	...	2 L
Cowmanure/compost	...	3 L
Leafmould	...	1 L
Oilcake (pulverised)	...	150g.
Mortar	...	400g
Super phosphate/Bonemeal	...	200g
Muriate of potash/Sulphate of potash	...	100g
Mag. Sulf	...	25 g.

6

Loam (medium)	...	10 litre
Humus	...	3 L
Mortar	...	500g
Fertilizer mixture	...	400g

Fertilizer mixture recommended for the compost No. 6 is given below. Any of them can be used with advantage.

1

Urea	...	250 g
Superphosphate	...	1 kg
Muriate of potash	...	300 g
Mag. sulph.	...	50 g

2

Ammonium sulphate	...	500 g
Super phosphate	...	1 kg.
Sulphate of potash/Muriate of potash	...	300 g.
Mag. sulph.	...	50 g.

3

Calcium ammonium nitrate (CAN)	...	250 g
Super phosphate	...	1 kg.
Muriate of potash	...	300 g
Mag. sulph.	...	50 g.

Mix all the ingredients of any of the potting compost (1-6) thoroughly and pile it in a moist condition for 2-3 weeks. The compost containing oil cake should be decomposed thoroughly before use. The compost thus seasoned should be sieved through 5mm. mesh twice. This process helps mix all the ingredients intimately and even a pinch of it will contain all the ingredients proportionately. Again pile the compost in a moist condition for few days. Seive the compost through 10mm mesh. This is now fit for using in pots for planting the saplings for bonsai.

It has already been said that a well-structured potting compost is needed for drainage and aeration. With the addition of humus in a considerable amount the potting compost becomes well structured. Some writers recommend to use riddles in the bottom layer of the pot, then coarse-grained soil in the middle layer an the fine-grained at the top. For which the potting soil is sieved through the sieves of different graded mesh. This is practically useless. Because it will remain effective for nearly six months only. But the improved structural condition of the potting compost helps maintain good drainage and aeration for years together. The potting compost of granular and friable structure is the best for the gardening purpose, may it be in pots or ground. A good quantity of humus in the soil improves the structural condition.

Potting

For making a standard bonsai the saplings are potted in the medium sized common pots. The shallow pots are not used in the early stage. Because in this stage the sapling should grow fast. The seedlings of the dicots grow a thick and long tap root which is not desirable in case of bonsai. If the seedling is potted in a deep pot the tap root grows larger than the laterals. At the time of shifting the tap root should be pruned nearly from base (as shows in illustration).

The drain hole/holes must be crocked as usual. First, place a pot shred on the hole with its concave side downwards. Then cover the crock with a layer of grit and coarse sand. This keeps the drain hole free, i.e. not chocked by the soil. The drain hole might be chocked from outside also if the pot is not placed above the ground. Generally bonsai pots are placed on the cemented floor. On the contrary if the bottom of the pot remains in contact with the ground the

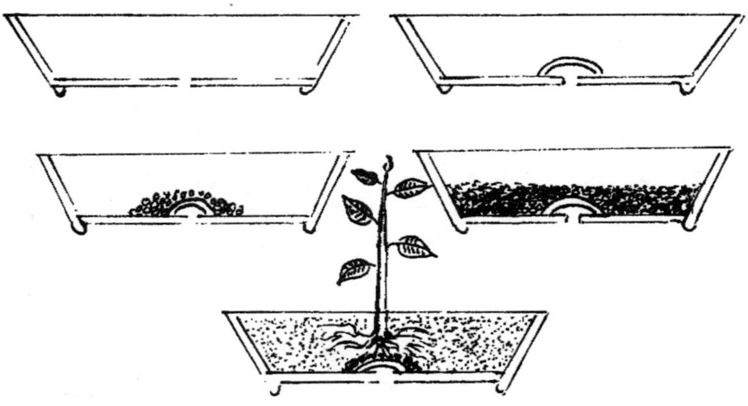

Fig. 94: *Potting*

weight of the pot exerts a pressure on the wet ground resulting in the rise of soil into the hole.

On crocking and putting aggregate on the crock the pot is filled with the potting compost up to two thirds the height. Then place the root ball of the sapling in the center of the pot and fill the sides with compost and press it as usual. At

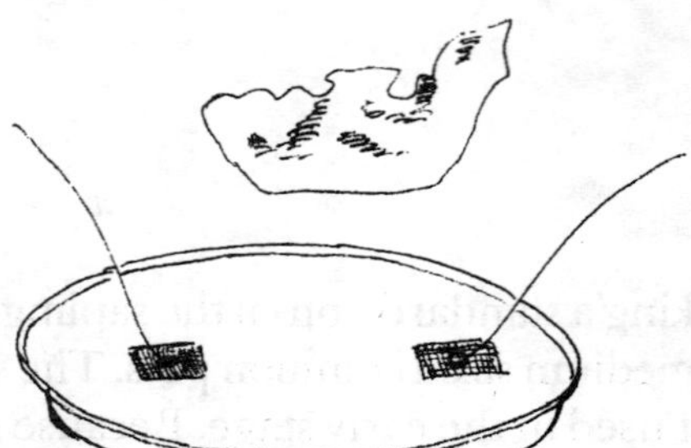

Fig. 94a: *This is how a rock is fixed to the pot*

the top an empty space is necessary to hold water while watering. So the pot should not completely be filled with the compost.

It should be borne in mind that the potting compost should be moist to facilitate handling at the time of potting. On potting water the plant copiously until a little water drains off through the drain hole. Staking might be necessary to keep the sapling erect. For this purpose a bamboo stick is inserted. Then the plant is tied to the stake with *sutli* (jute twine). If the bare-root sapling is potted it should be kept in shade for a week or so until the roots take soil.

Step-By-Step Developments

A little sapling may grow to a well-shaped bonsai through different cultural operations and training. Here the step by step developments are discussed with illustrations. Obviously the figures are more helpful than the tips.

1. To make it bushy a branching system must be thick. An umbrella-like spreading head is desired in most cases. To achieve this the tips of the sapling are pinched off successively from the early stage as shown in the figures. In the later stage the twigs are clipped to give a desired shape.
2. The first stopping will force to sprout a number of shoots-one from each leaf axil. All of them are not retained. The number of branches to be retained and their respective position are dependent on the trunk style.

Fig. 95: *Step-by-step developments*

Root Pruning Shifting or Repotting

When the soil ball of the pot becomes root-bound first shifting to the large pot becomes necessary. Generally the root pruning is not necessary before the first shifting. If the tap root grows long and thick it needs to be pruned to accommodate the root system in the shallow pot designed for the bonsai. The plant grown in a shallow pot is likely to be pushed up by the matted network of roots formed in between the pot and the soil. This is found invariably in case of the monocots, especially the date palm. The monocots grow fibrous roots. But in pots they are found to grow spirally like a long rope. When the soil ball is pushed up high due to the matted root growth the quantity of soil become less than the total volume of the roots. It is then root pruning and shifting or repotting become imperative.

In case of the first shifting root pruning is not adopted. Because shifting is done to a pot of larger dimensions. It becomes root-bound and the shoot growth retards consequently. The new pot to which the plant will be shifted must be crocked for the passage of excess water. But this time pot shreds are not used. Pieces of copper wire netting or nylon netting are used instead. Cover the hole/holes with a cut piece of netting and the netting is covered with grit so that the potting compost cannot chock the netting. The grits of required dimensions can be obtained by sieving coarse sand. The grits of sand is known as *Kankar*. Now fill the pot with potting compost proportionately to form the

base of the root ball of the plant to be potted. Take out the plant with its roots ball as usual. If the thickness of the ball is more that cannot be accommodated in the shallow pot prune the roots with a pair of scissors as shown in the illustration. Then place it vertically in the middle of the pot and fill the sides with compost and press it as usual. Water copiously after potting.

Re-potting is necessary when the plant needs fresh compost. Root pruning is done simultaneously. In this case the size of the pot is not changed. In the process of root pruning one thirds of the soil ball is reduced. In this condition the tree with the remaining root ball is repotted using fresh potting compost. The proper time for repotting is considered the rains or early spring.

Root pruning is not a difficult operation. One thirds of the root ball from the outer side is removed. A pair of sharp scissors is used for this purpose. In the chapter dealing with tools and implements the cutting tools together with the scissors have been described and illustrated. If any thick root is to be reduced use secateurs or tensor saw.

Fig. 96:
Root prunning

Another type of root pruning has been innovated by the author adopting which the root ball need not be taken out. Pushing a sharp knife through the root ball 3-4 cm away from the rim the root is cut parallel to the rim thus forming a circle. The soil with the cut pieces of roots is completely removed and the void is filled with the fresh potting compost. In the ground the monocots have one type of roots which is fibrous. But in pots they grow two types of roots which is fibrous and the other is very long which form a coil at the bottom of the pot where there is no soil.. Nevertheless they grow fast. The coil of roots form a cushion-like soilless stratum. When it becomes thick the root ball of the pot is pushed up high. For repotting the cushion of roots should be removed.

Fig. 97:
Root prunning by a new technique innovated by the author

Fixing Large Bonsai to A Shallow Pot

A full-sized bonsai in a very small container runs the risk of being knocked down or blown over. As a remedy it is fixed to the pot by a tying device. Push some wire through the drain holes so that it can be used later to secure the plant in its place.

The process of passing wire through the drain holes is likely to displace the crocks resulting in the soil trickling out. To guard against this, instead of crocks small squares of wire netting are used. The wire will conveniently pass through the netting without displacing it. For draining off water nettings are found to serve better than the crocks. The two ends of the wire will help secure the plant in its shallow pot. If monocots are grown in common bonsai pots this process of fixing is a must.

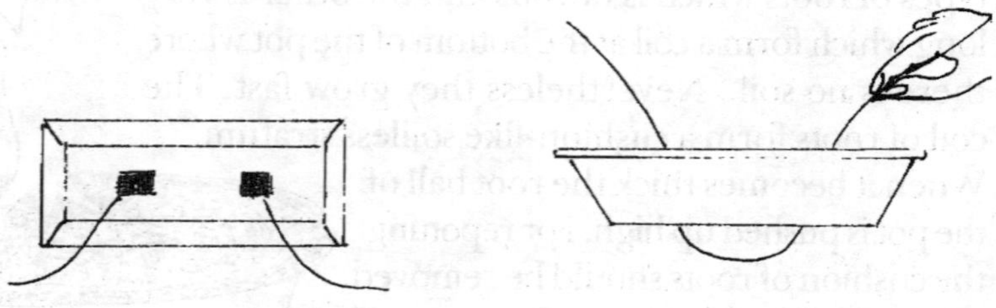

Fig. 98:
The wire secures the tree in a shallow pot

Methods of Dwarfing

It is obvious that a bonsai is made dwarf. So it should not grow fast. The technique should be such as to dwarfing the tree. The tap root is the large and thicker than any other roots. If the tap root is allowed to grow unchecked the top of the plant will also grow straight. In other words the branching system is correspondingly the same as the root system which is shown in the illustration. If the branches are spreading the lateral root system will also be spreading. The root system of 'Gulmohor' (*Delonix regia*) and Deodar (*Polyathi alongifolia*) cannot be the same. The former is spreading and the later long and cylindrical. If a tall growing plant is made dwarf by regular pruning its root system will correspond to the shape of the branches.

First, the roots must be confined to the limited space of a pot. If the roots pass through the drain hole and find the ground to grow the shoot will begin to grow fast correspondingly. Therefore the bonsai pots must be placed on the cemented floor of the conservatory or on the brick-lined terrace. In the rains the roots of some plants such as the member of the *Ficus* family are found to grow fast outside the pot though there is no soil. In this case the roots not only pass through the drain holes but also cross the rim of the pot to touch the floor. Therefore the periodical checking to stop the unwanted root growth is imperative.

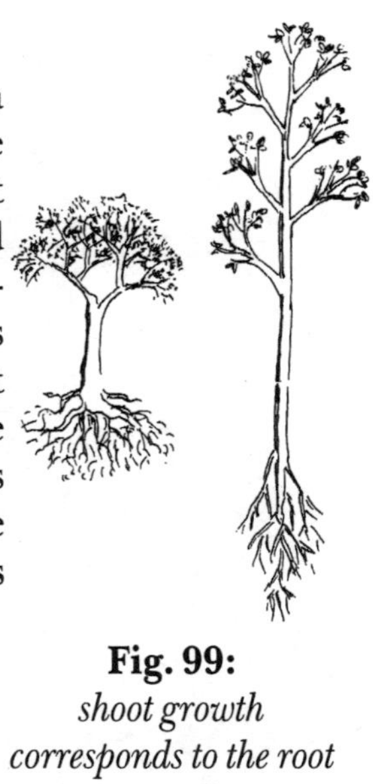

Fig. 99: *shoot growth corresponds to the root growth*

Regular pruning keeps the plant in a dwarf state. But all types of bonsai are not bushy. In that case the branches are selected and allowed to grow, and the others are removed.

For dwarfing leaf pruning is resorted to. The details have been discussed in Chapter 21.

Feeding with nitrogenous manure and fertilizer should be restricted. Because nitrogen stimulates the shoot and root growths. It makes the internodes long and the leaves large. Nitrogen in the chemical forms are very quick acting. Hence the useless for bonsai. The organic forms of nitrogen in a very limited dose is recommended for bonsai. Because it helps maintain the slow vegetative growth but ensures flowering and fruiting. Because carbohydrate and nitrogen ratio (C : N) in the plant tissues should be such as to show the preponderance of carbohydrates.

Watering Weeding and Feeding

WATERING

The bonsai tree is larger than its pot. So the soil is comperatively less than what is normally required. For this reason the soil runs dry quickly. So the grower should be watchful to meet the water requirement of the miniature trees.

The general rule is to water when the soil tends to dry. This will help cause aeration of the soil, which is necessary for the respiration of the roots. Watering with a water can fitted with a fine spout is convenient. The forceful water jetted out of the hose pipe would wash away the mulch together with the surface soil. If a hose pipe is used it must be fitted with a fine rose for a shower-like pouring of water.

Generally watering is needed once a day, which should be done in the morning. In summer the need of water is more, so watering is needed more than once. If the grower is not more watchful the plant might be affected due to the shortage of water during the hoter period of summer. So the method that ensures automatically the steady supply of water might be adopted. One of them is the capillary method. In this method water rises upwards from

below as oil rises through the wick of a lamp. By the second method water is supplied by dripping from a plastic tubing. The thin hose pipe is connected with a water tap. The other end is closed. The pipe passes along the row of bonsai pots touching the base of the trees. Near each base a pinhole is made to drip water for soaking the pot soil. It is obvious,

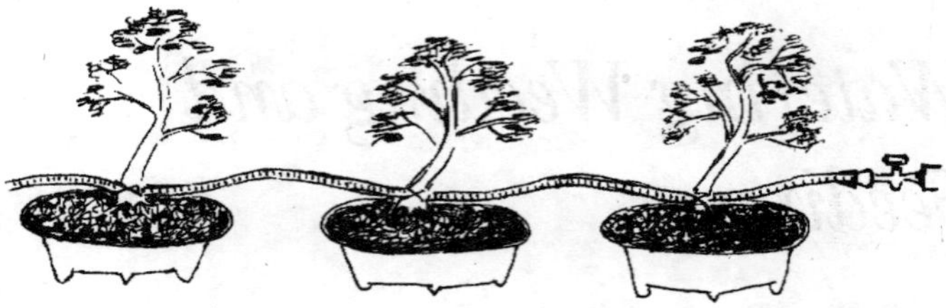

Fig. 100: *Watering by a drip method*

when more water is not required the tap is closed.

Fig. 101: *Watering by capillary method*

For the capillary method of watering the bonsai pot is placed in a pot of shallow water so as to immerse half of the pot. Water will rise through the drain hole and soak the soil gradually. Water rises vertically through the pores of the soil particles as oil rises through the pores of the wick of a lamp. The rise of liquid through the minute or capillary pores is known as 'capillary rise of liquid'. The process is used to soak the soil of the pot. During the excessively hot and dry days of summer the small bonsai pots may need frequent waterings even twice or thrice a day. To cope with the situation a bonsai pot is placed in a larger pot which is filled with water once a day at 9-10 a.m.

Fig. 102: *Wetting the trunk with capillary method*

When the whole family is out for holidaying watering bonsai pots creates problem. The solutions are found in the ways e.g. by drip method (already discussed) and the wick soaking method which supplies water to the stem (not to the pot soil) by a strap-like wick. One end of the wick is dipped in a glass of water and the other end is wound round the base of the stem. The water of the glass will rise to the stem through the wick by the capillary method. Until the water of the glass is consumed the plant will be getting water. But this is not capable of supplying water directly to the root by soaking the soil. In the drip method to allow a slow flow of water the stop cock of the tap is turned half or even more as needed.

WEEDING

Bonsai, unlike other garden subjects, is not troubled by weeds. In other words the weed growth is not found rampant in bonsai pots. Generally during the rainy months if the pots are exposed to the full sun weeds grow that should be uprooted in the early stage. Many growers like to cover the surface soil with a layer of sphagnum moss. This is obviously very unfavourable for the weed growth. Bonsai grows well under the agro-shade net. The sun light that filters through it does not encourage the weed growth.

FEEDING

For supplementary feeding applying top dressing or liquid manure is in practice. But the sufficient space for top dressing in a shallow pot is wanting. For this reason instead of applying top dressing of fertilizer mixture the potting compost is used. To make a room for it the top soil is loosened by forking and removed proportionately. On the contrary applying liquid manure is simple, i.e. no hoeing, nor removing soil is necessary. The main ingredients of a liquid manure should be oil cake. Any chemical nitrogen fertilizer like urea, ammonium sulphate, calcium ammonium nitrate etc. should not be used. But for the fruit bearing trees it might be used with advantage.

1

Oil cake (mustard/ground nut)	...	100 g
D A P (Di-ammonium phosphate)	...	50 g
Wood ash	...	25 g
Magnesium sulphate	...	10 g
Water	...	10 L

2

Oil cake (mustard/groundnut)	...	100 g
Suphala 15:15:15	...	50 g
Magnesium sulphate	...	10 g
Water	...	10 L

Soak oil cake in five litres of water for 8-10 days. Make a solution of other ingredients only 6-10 hours before use. Mix both the liquids and add water to it to make a solution of 10 litre. Apply any of the liquid manures thus prepared in 10-15 pots. Water the pots 30 minutes before applying liquid manure.

A bonsai, like other garden plants, needs the supplement of micronutrients such as iron, zinc, boron, molybdenum etc. The mixture of micronutrients are available in the market. They are sold in the proprietary names, e.g. Multiplex, Agromin, Tracel-2, Vipul etc. Micronutrients or trace elements are also fed through the foliage. For this purpose any proprietary product of mitronutrients are sprayed with water on the foliage when the plant is growing (not dormant).

Spray only twice at a month's interval in a year. Besides biostimulants can be used like the foliar feed. There are a number of proprietary products marketed by their manufacturers. Any of them can be tried with advantage. A biostimulent helps translocate the synthesized products from leaves to the stem and roots rapidly. As a result the stems and branches become thicker early. The whole amount of the product of the carbon assimilation should be translocated before the leaves fall in winter. Not only that if the translocation process is more rapid than usual the manufacturing process of the products will be accelerated. In that case the woody parts of the tree will be thicker very rapidly. A biostimulant should be sprayed on the foliage not more than thrice in a year starting from June to November at the interval of 8 weeks. The following is a list of biostimulants with the name of their manufactures.

Products	*Manufacturers*
Miraculan	National Organic Chemicals Ltd.
Aminos	Rallis India Ltd.
Paras Photosynth	Hindustan Lever Ltd.
Biozyme	Wockhardt Ltd.
Arogen	Pharma-flora India

Different Styles

The bonsai of many shapes are there. Those shapes are the imitations of nature. In other words, the old trees of the different shapes are found in nature. To make a bonsai a particular shape is imitated and that style is designated accordingly. First, their classification and then their characteristics with growing techniques have been discussed. On the basis of the height they are again classified as Miniature bonsai, Small bonsai, Medium bonsai and large bonsai of the shapes of the trunk and branching system. Groves, rural landscapes and the forest scene are also imitated in growing bonsai.

TREES OF DIFFERENT HEIGHTS

1. Miniature Bonsai : A very little pot, a little bigger than a tea plate, is used for this type of bonsai. The height of a miniature tree should not exceed 15cm.
2. Small Bonsai : The bonsai of 20-25 cm. height are grouped in this class.
3. Medium Bonsai : The bonsai of 25-30 cm. height are called 'medium bonsai'.
4. Large Bonsai : 30-90 cm. high old trees are known as 'large bonsai'.

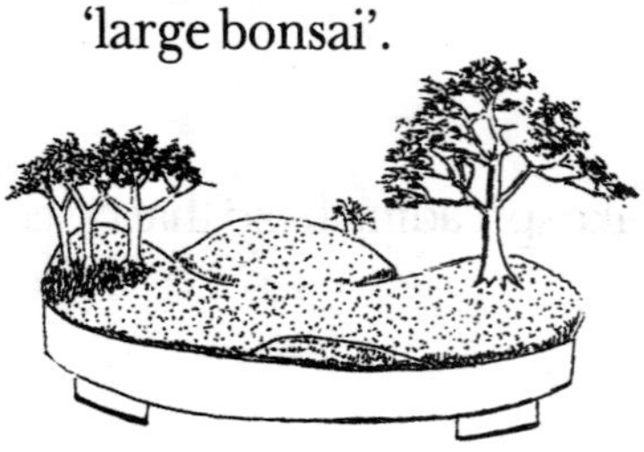

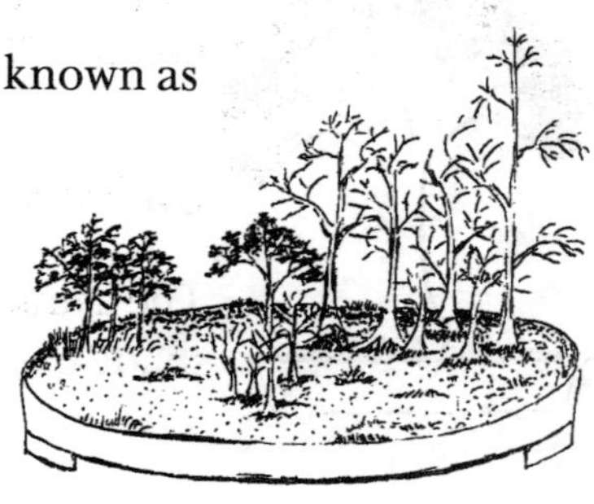

STYLES

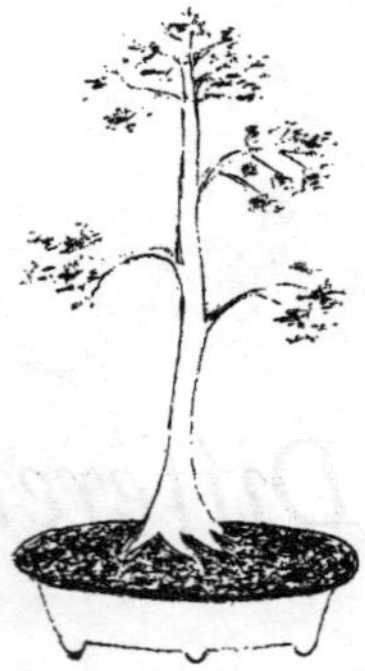

Formal upright

The trunk is erect with branches growing symmetrically in all directions, but the front of the tree is kept free from branches upto two thirds the length.

Informal upright

The trunk is erect but with few curves. The curvature is gradually smaller towards the top.

Twisted trunk

The trunk twists round and round on itself. The branches might grow in any direction.

Long bare-root

Roots like the stem, remain exposed. Only their growing tips remain in the ground. In this case the thick roots look like the continuation of the stem. This is to imitate the mangrove plants whose roots are found exposed due to the tidal effect.

Broom

The upright stem with broom-like shoots which are allowed to grow at a certain height. They are more or less crowded.

Umbrella

The trunk having an umbrella-like spreading head that casts shade over a wide area.

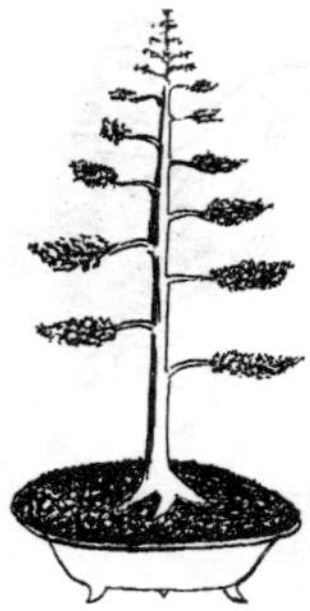

Conical

Remarkably upright and slender tree that looks like a cypress.

Spherical

A spherical crown on the upright trunks.

Slanting

The trunk is inclined more or less to an angle of 45°.

The branches grow in all directions. The thick roots are exposed in the direction of inclination.

Literati

Trunk grows in an informal upright style or slightly inclined. The branches are only in the top third. Significance: Wise enough to find peace by discarding the touch of the earthly things. So the branches grow away from the earth.

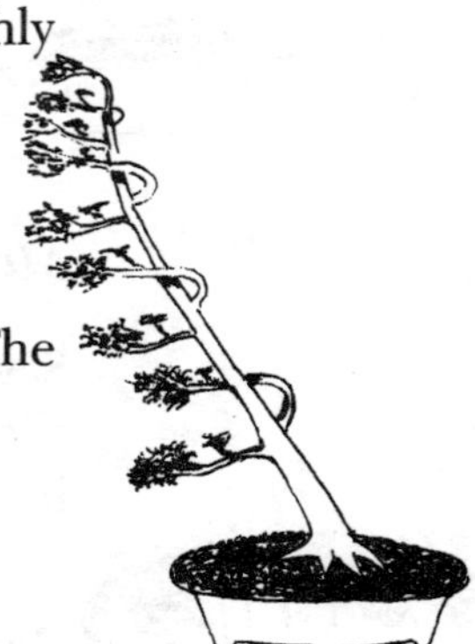

Windswept

The appearance resembles a tree as if lashed by a gale. The branches and twigs as if forced to take one direction.

Semi-cascade

The form is to imitate a plant growing horizontally on a cliff. The top of the tree lies below the line of the rim of the pot.

Cascade

The form resembles the tree that hangs down low over a rock. The trunk and branches of the bonsai hang down well across the base of a usually tall pot.

Twin trunk

Two trunks of different girth, growing from one root but their style being the same.

Clump

Several trunks more or less of the same size forming a group. They grow from a root

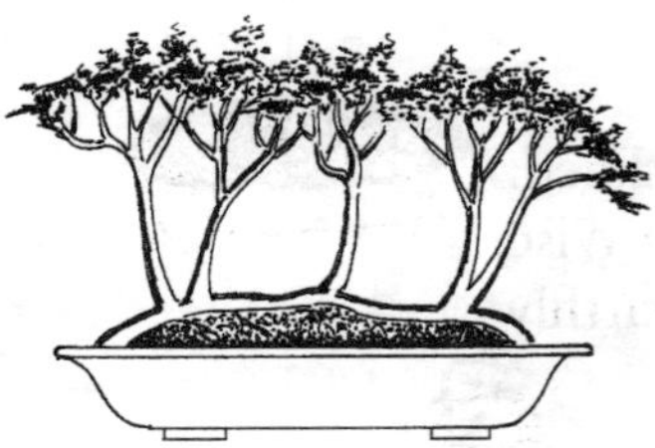

Raft

The trunk buried horizontally in a pot, which grows root downwards and a number of shoots upwards each of which resembling a person standing on a raft.

Multi-tree

Several miniature trees of the same species but of different ages grown in a shallow and circular pot.

Rock-grown

Tree or trees growing in small hollows or crevices of a rock.

Root-over-rock

Tree sitting on the top the rock sends out the roots to soil in the pot.

Training of Bonsai

Not only the process of dwarfing but also that of training is needed to make a bonsai. The age-old tree with its beautiful grotesque form is very attractive, which has to be brought about artificially in bonsai. The nature of training depends upon the style to be imitated, i.e. to give a particular shape found in a old tree in nature. A type of trunk with its branching system is represented by a style. Many such styles have been discussed with figures in the preceeding chapter. They are designated with the suitable nomenclature. Obviously the training should start with a particular style in view. In other words the training is to give the shape of a particular style.

In the beginning select the style then bring the plant in the level of the eye to fix which side be the fornt of the tree. Because in the front no branch should project to the viewers. But towards the top no restriction is there, i.e. the branches are allowed in all directions. If so done the frontal view will look better. In other words, the beauty of the style of the specimen is manifested better at frontage. The following operations are needed to give the desired shape.

DISBUDDING

In the process of dwarfing the disbudding is a common practice, which consists of pinching off the leaf buds. This process makes the plant bushy as it forces to sprout a good number of shoots. In case of the miniature bonsai disbudding is done more frequently. The main objective of

disbudding is to force the shoots from the leaf joints just below the pinched top. To conform with the branching system of the adopted style branching is forced in the early stage of the sapling. Hence the necessity of disbudding. On forcing by disbudding a pair of laterals emerge from the axils of the twin leaves. Select one of them. In the lower set if the left-side branch is retained, for the next set retain the branch of the right side and so on, i.e. in a zigzag pattern. In doing so there should be no branch directing the front. But there is no restriction for the back side. At the top however, the branches should be in all directions.

PRUNING

Fig. 125: *Pruning with concave cutting pliers*

Pruning of branches or shoots is required in the later stages of growth. The cutting point is selected and cut with a sharp pruning knife or a pair of secaterus. For bonsai, however, a special tool is used, which is concave cutting pliers. This cutter makes the cut surface concave which hastens the healing, i.e. it quickens the growth of the bark to cover the cut surface.

The stem of the sapling if elongated needs to be pruned. Bear in mind that a very thick stem transversely cut across may have the shape of a bonsai in a very short time. As that cut will bear the scar mark oddly without any change till to the last that specimen can never be regarded as a good bonsai. Obviously a sharp pair of secateurs is used for cutting branches.

WIRING

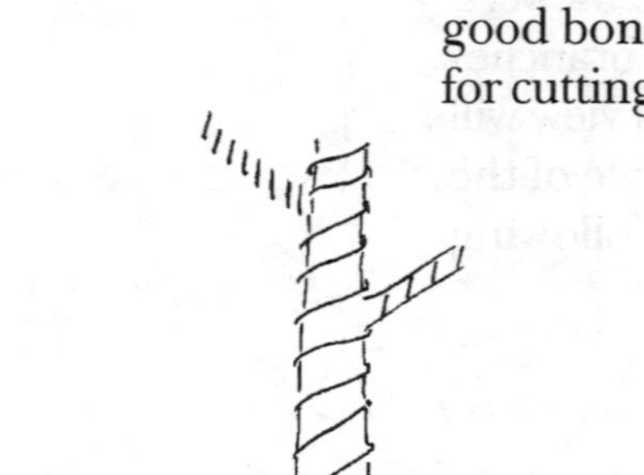

Fig. 126: *Wire is wound for bending*

To give the desired shape to the stems or branches bending or curving is needed. There are many means by which it is done. Wring is one of them. A straight branch can be bent by winding wire. According to the thickness of the stem or branch the thickness of the wire should correspond. In other words for bending a thin branches a thin wire has to be used. Generally copper wire is used but galvanised wire too might be used. The process of winding is just as shown in the illustration. The wire

should not be wound lightly because it may cut through the bark. On wiring bend the branch as needed. It should be borne in mind that a wiring must not last more than a period of eight weeks. Because it weekens the plant. After removing the wire the plant should be kept in a shade for a week or so. Wiring can be repeated for 2-3 times but a gap of 6 months must be there between the two attempts.

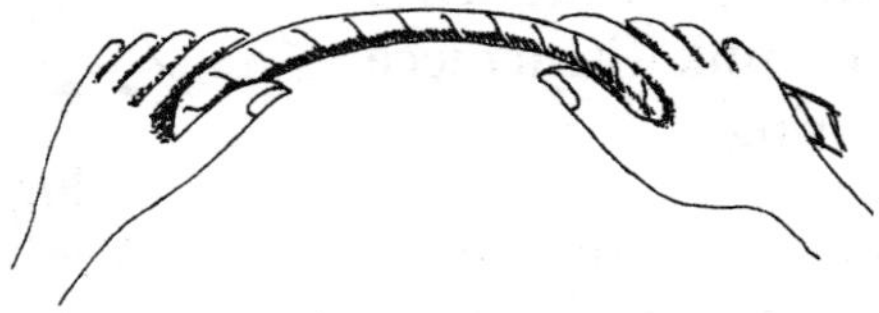

Fig. 127: *Bending after wiring*

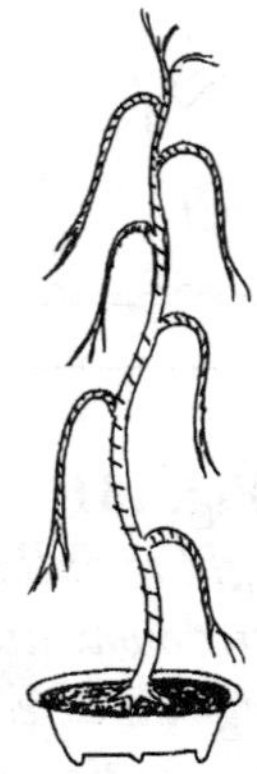

Fig. 128: *Wire to a weeping willow style*

Bending by a jack

To bend a branch at particular point use a bending jack. A type of small jack is available in the market. One may get it manufactured in a welder's shop. A screw is fitted to a clamp. The clamp is fixed to a point of the branch, the screw is extended to exert a pressure at the point to be bent. In other words by increasing the length of the screw between the clamp and the branch the necessary pressure is exerted on the branch to bend. The pressure should be increased gradually. Due to the pressure the tip of the screw may cause injury on the branch at the point of contact. Put a pad of cotton between the screw and the branch to prevent the direct contact.

OTHER METHODS

Besides these there are other methods which are comparatively easy. With the help of these methods the branches are made horizontal. The branches of the young trees grow vertically but with the age they gradually become horizontal, i.e. they change the direction of their growth. This is done artificially in case of bonsai.

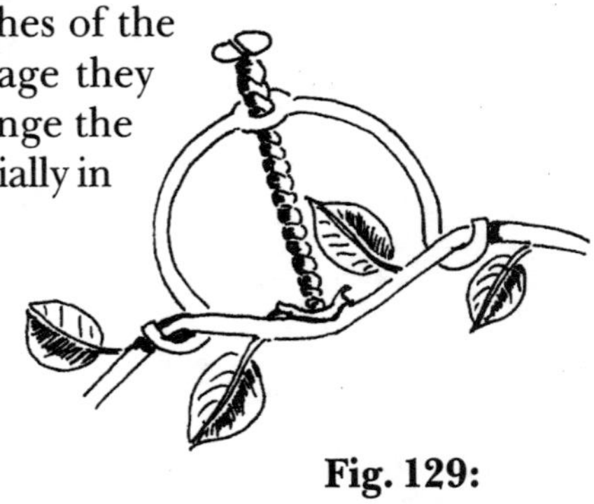

Fig. 129: *Bending with a jack*

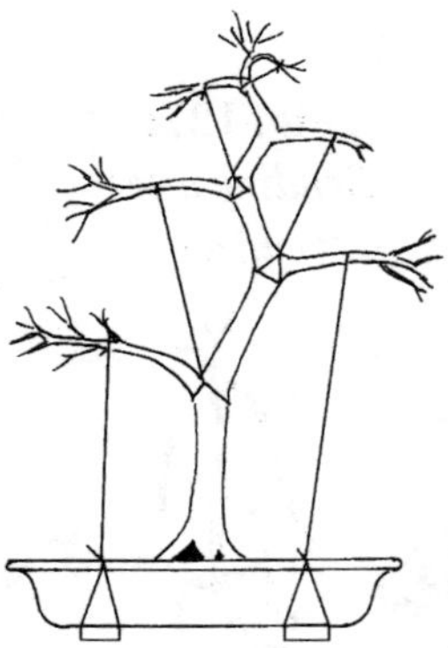

Fig. 131:
Weight to pull a branch downwards. To change the direction branches are tied to the trunk or pot

1. The branch is bent with the weight of stone of suitable dimensions. A piece of nylon sting is used to hand the stone from the branch as shown in the figure.
2. By this method the branch is tied to the trunk with a piece of nylon string.
3. Instead of tying to the trunk the string can be tied to the pot to bend the branch/branches downwards.
4. Using a piece of wood the branches are bent apart.
5. Week branches are pulled towards the stronger one and tied to it.

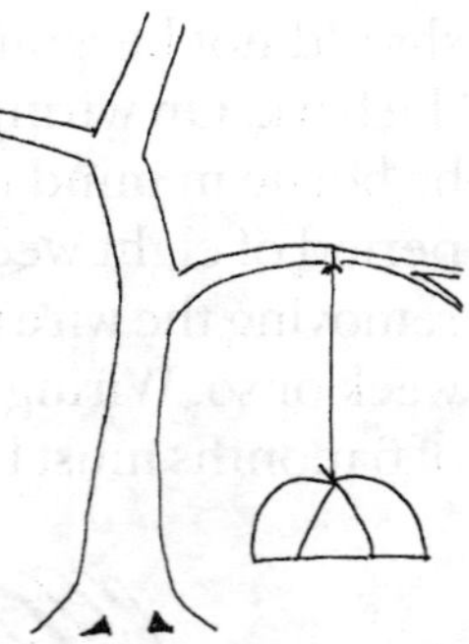

Fig. 130:
Weight to pull a branch downwards

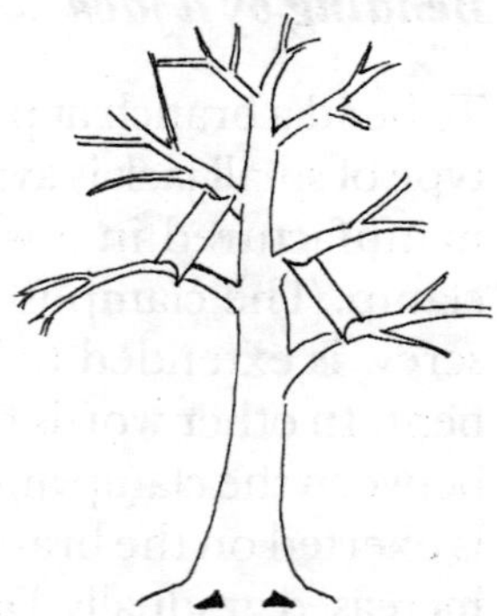

Fig. 132:
Using a piece of wood to bend the branch apart

Fig. 132a:
Initially bare roots are tied to the rock

Tools Implements and Accessories

Some tools and accessories are required for growing bonsai. Some of them are for different cultural operations and others for training and pruning. A list of implements, tools and accessories is given below.

1. Sieves : Strainers of meshes of different sizes are available. For sieving potting compost 4mm x 4mm mesh is suitable. For sieving sand for separating grits the same sieve is useful. For preparing seed compost the use of 2mm x 2mm mesh is recommended.

2. Small Pruning Scissors : It should be sharp. The handle is larger than the pair of scissors. This is suitable for pruning fibrous roots.

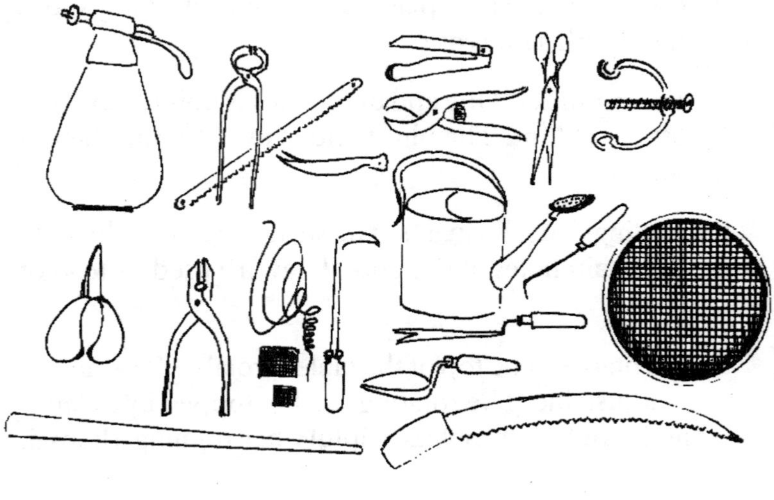

Fig. 133: *Tools and accessories*

3. Secateurs : A tool for rose pruning. It is also useful for pruning branches or thick roots of bonsai.

4. Concave Cutting Pliers : It is a special tool as it has no other use expect for cutting the branches of bonsai. On cutting it leaves a concave cut surface that heals up quickly. It is imported from abroad.

5. Wire Cutter : The tool is also known as 'Plus'. It should be suitable for cutting thin wires say, 12-15 gauges.

6. Wires : Copper or galvanised wires of different gauges, say 12-20 gauges. It is to be borne in mind that the higher the gauge the thinner is the thickness.

7. Leaf cutter : For cutting leaves or leaflets of dicots.

8. Pruning Saw : A small curved saw used for pruning comparatively thick branches.

9. Tensor Saw : Its blade and the handle can be separated. Only the blade portion of the saw is used to prune the thick tap root.

10. Jack : This tool is used to bend a portion of the branch. The clamp is fixed to a point of the branch. The screw is protruded to exert a pressure on the point of the branch to bend.

11. Common Implements : Garden trowels, hoeing forks, *niranis, khurpis* etc.

12. Cans : Water cans, plastic or metal, with long spout fitted with a fine rose.

13. Potting sticks : One end of the stick is pointed and the other is blunt. The blunt end is used to ram the pot soil.

14. Nettings : Small squares of mesh, nylon or wire, to cover the drain holes of the pots. They are used instead of crocks.

15. Turntable : The top of the table is rotable. The height is adjustable. The rotating can be stopped by a clamp as desired. Such table is helpful while training a bonsai.

Flowering and Fruit Bearing Bonsai

In this country fruit-bearing bonsai is very popular. On the show benches the bonsai of lime, orange, guava, karanda, mulberry, carambola, ber etc. with their heavy bearing are very common. The bonsai of mulberry is found to bear fruits and flowers almost throughout the year. But the flowering bonsai is rarely seen. However orange (sweet or sour), kamquat lime, pomelo bear plenty of sweet-scented flowers in February-March. The flowering bonsai illustrated in INDOOR BONSAI of Paul Lesniewicz are very charming which are hardly found in other works oriental or occidental. However in case of fruiting bonsai the pots used are larger than usual.

In the season preceeding the flowering watering must be restricted, i.e. less water should be given to retard the vegetative growth. As for example, lime, lemon or orange should not be forced to grow by supplementary feeding or normal watering from November till the fruit setting. On fruit setting feeding and normal watering should be restored.

Supplementary feeding with phosphate, potash, magnesium and a little nitrogen should be done six months before the flowering season. It should be borne in mind that the deficiency of phosphate and potash will not encourage flowering and fruiting. To stop the flower and fruit drop apply auxin by spraying. The proprietary product Planofix (0.5cc/L) is extensively used for this purpose. There are other products containing auxin are also available in the market.

Bonsai of Attractive Foliage

Bonsai with healthy foliage look bright. The foliage must be kept insect and disease free. The leaves with insect bites should be removed. The leaves partly damaged by disease infection should also be removed. The dust deposits can be washed away by showering water from the rose of a water can or by the forceful jet of a hose pipe. During the rains the natural showers prevent dust deposits. But in other seasons the air pollution leaves a dirty incrustation on the leaves. So frequent cleansing is necessary. The leaves that have been discoloured due to age should be removed.

LEAF PRUNING

Practically leaf pruning is needed to make a bonsai dwarf, because it checks the normal growth of the plant. It must be judiciously practised as it weakens the plant. The species which has large leaves such as rubber, guava, mulberry and banyan is subjected to leaf pruning which reduces the size of the lamina or leaf blade.

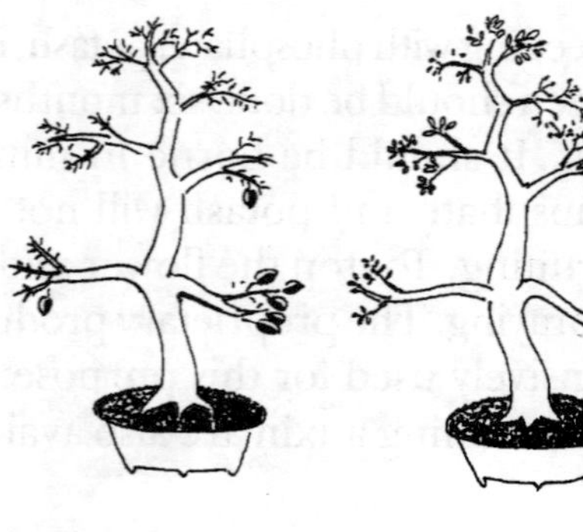

Fig. 134: *Leaf pruning*

Generally leaf pruning is practised once a year in July-August. It is needed for the aged plants which still bear normal-sized leaves. While pruning cut away the leaf blade leaving the whole leaf stalk. Hardly one week after the operation the leaf stalks will turn yellow and fall. Then new leaf buds will sprout from the leaf joints. If so considered, all leaves may not be removed at a time. At the time of pruning the age of the leaves should not be less than 2-4 months. Never touch the tender leaves.

To expose the grotesque structure of the branching system one may resort to reducing the leaves. In the deciduous form the bonsai should not be exhibited. If the leaves are pruned two months before the date of exhibition the exhibits will be adorned with the tender foliage. In winter shows the bonsai of the deciduous species hardly has any glamour. But it can be forced to put forth new buds and foliage if placed for few weeks in a hot house.

Displaying

In this country, unlike Japan, bonsai is reared in the conservatory and displayed occasionally in the verandah, living room or dining room. Because a permanent suitable alclove exclusively for the bonsai is not added to our house. In Japan, however, such alclove is known as 'Tokonoma' which is used exclusively for bonsai or *ikebana*,

The bonsai are displayed in a manner in which one of them plays an important roll such as to form a focal point. All other materials should be just to complement and enhance the beauty of the scene and accentuate the focal point. If there are two trees of the same height one of them is intended to be the focal point.

The soil surface of the bonsai pot should be covered with greens which may bear tiny flowers. The herbs with small leaves and prostrated stems can be used for this purpose. But the grass-like pattern is better that lends itself to create an effect of meadows, especially in the cluster planting which is to make a forest scene. Because the forest meadow has a special charm. The lush green growth of a meadow needs the direct sun more than usual.

A cascade or semi-cascade bonsai should be displayed in a tall stand. It would be better if there are three in number-one is larger than the two which are equal in size and form. Those cascades are displayed side by side with the larger one at the middle and at a higher level.

Bonsai should not be conjested, i.e. enough space be allowed between them. The stand should be proportionate, i.e. the stout and strong stand should be used for the large specimens. The height of the stand should nearly be double the height of the pot. These might be an exception in case of the cascade bonsai. The colour of the background should be light, e.g.. off white, light cream, light blue etc. The base table is polished with dark brown or black colour. In the exhibition the show benches should be covered with the cloth of sand colour. The height of the bench should nearly be 1.5 metre.

The additional plants of the low height are used to complement the beauties of the main specimens. The herbs with various sizes, shapes and colours of the foliage are used for this purpose. They are grown in the shallow containers or trays of bottle green colour. The herbaceous plants suitable for this purpose have been dealt with in a preceeding chapter.

Besides plants trays with beautiful stones and water are also displayed with bonsai in Japan. In the Japanese terminology it is know as *SUISEKI* which is coined with two words, *Sui* and *Seki* meaning water and stone respectively. To give a natural touch the presence of stone, water and meadow are essential. The stones are collected from the river beds or valleys. Those which have sculptured form naturally or chiseled are selected. They are to represent the rocks, clips and mountains as found in nature. A good *Suiseki*, like bonsai, should have a definite front, back, sides and apex. The conception of the Japanese water garden is exhibited by *Suiseki* beside the bonsai. It should be borne in mind that *Suiseki* should not be placed in front of the bonsai. Generally a bonsai is placed between two trays, one having the complementary plants or grass and the other containing *Suiseki*. The grass-tray is in the front but in the lower level, and *Suiseki* in the back thus creating a complete scene that features a distant mountain with a close-up view of meadow at the front.

Fig. 135: *Suiseki*

Pest and Disease Control

Bonsai, like other plants, might be affected by pests and diseases. Obviously the plant diseases are caused by fungi, bacteria or vires. They are mostly microscopic. In other words, they are hardly seen with the naked eyes. The infection of a disease may not be seen until the symptoms are manifested. Therefore the preventive measures are very efficatious than the curative. To prevent the disease infection apply fungicides at least four times a year at regular intervals. Fungicides are mainly classified into three groups, e.g. the zinc based, copper based (contact fungicides) and systemic. On application the later is absorbed by the plant bodies and gives protection to the plant from within. On the contrary the contact fungicides kill the fungus spores on contact. Therefore to cover a broad spectrum three types of fungicides are sprayed alternately.

The disease may cause a serious damage to your plants. In some cases the infected parts might be destroyed causing a sort of mutilation. Dieback is one of them. So take care of the disease infection. In case the preventive measure are not full-proof take the remedial measure as soon as the disease symptoms are seen. Many disease-causing fungi come from the ground. So keep your bonsai on the bench of at least 60cm. height. The insect infestation is less in bonsai. As they are kept apart from other vegetations of the garden the migration of insect is minimized. But it cannot be applicable in case of the winged insects. Some insects are microscopic which are not conspicuously visible. So the growers should know the symptoms of their attack. Thrips and mites are quoted as examples. In anticipation of the insect attack no preventive measure is taken by spraying. But to prevent soil insects like termites, earthworms, nematodes etc. systemic insecticides like Furadan, Thimate, Sevidol etc. are used periodically at a regular interval.

INSECTS

Aphids

Black or brown winged insects grow in thousands and suck the sap of the growing tips, soft foliage and flower buds. Spraying with nicotine sulphate or tobacco-leaf imulsion controls the insects.

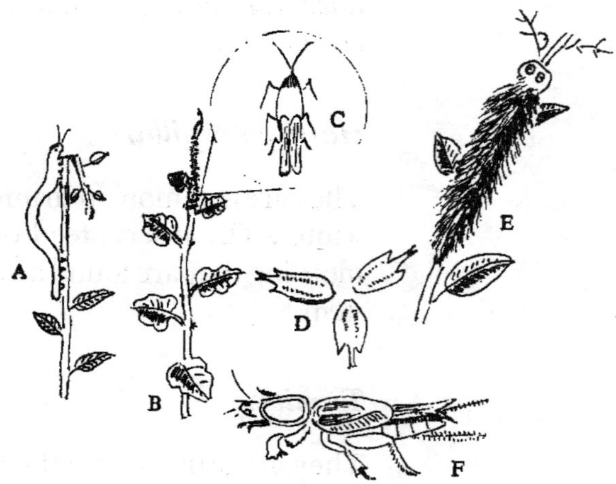

Fig. 136: Insects
A- Caterpillar
B- Aphids
C- One individual magnified
D- Mealy bugs
E- Hairy caterpillar
F- Mole cricket

Thrips

A minute insects suck the sap from the leaves which curl and dry at tips.

Control: Malathion (2ml/L), Sevin (dust) or Rogor (2ml/L)

Mies

The minute insects remain on the lower surface of the leaves and suck their sap resulting in the pale-yellow appearance.

Control: Dusting the plant with flour of sulphur (25g/10sq.m) or spraying cold water in the evening on the lower surface of the leaves.

Leaf-cutting caterpillars

They feed on voraciously on leaves. Collection and destroying the egg masses and hand picking of the large individuals are an effective control.

Chemical control : Metacid 50(2ml/L) or Malathion (2ml/L) or Monocil (2ml/L) spray.

Mealy bugs

A soft-bodied insect covered with a white or brown powder-like substance suck the sap from the tender parts of the plant. They secret a honey-like substance from their body which attracts the ants. The adults hardly move. The infestation spreads mainly by ants. Collect the egg masses deposited on the leaves and destroy. The adults should be removed by hand picking.

Chemical control: Malathion (2ml/L) or Metasystocks (1ml/l) spray.

Hairy caterpillars

They are common on drumstick plants in autumn to early winter. The insects feed on the foliage at night. In the morning they are found assembled on the lower part of the stem.

Termites

They are attracted by the organic substances of the soil. Termites destroy soil humus and then roots and stems.

Control: Darsban or Pyriban can be used against termites.

Mole crickets (Gryllotalpa vulgaris)

They cause harm to seeds and seedlings. They are attracted by the organic-matters of the soil. They make burrows as they pass just below the soil surface.

Control: As recommended against termites.

Earthworms

The earthworm multiplies in soil with plenty of humus. The young individuals feed on the growing roots and the injury caused thereby is susceptible to the disease infection.

Control: As recommended against termites. The application of *Mahua* oil cake in the diluted form can destroy earthworms. The solution of permanganate of potash can be applied to kill earthworms. The granular insecticides like Furadan, Phorate etc. are very poisonuous to the earthworm.

Scale insect

The scale form circular incrustations of reddish brown colour on the stem. The infestation occurs from the base upwards. The heavy infestation forms scarfy incrustations of an unsightly appearance. Each small scale represents an individual which sticks to the plant. The adult insect cannot move. In their young stage they crawl to the nearly plants.

Control: Spray Malathion or Sevin.

Leaf rolling larva

It is a larva of an insect. It feeds on flower buds, then rolls the leaves for making its shelter.

Control : Malathion or Metasytox is used to check the insect.

Leaf miner

It is the larva of a certain type of moth. The citrus leaves especially those of lime are affected by leafminer. The mining habit is confind to the larval stage of the insect. The larva destroys the tissues of the leaves which get distorted and become unsightly.

Control: It is controlled by spraying with Malathion, Lindane or applying nicotine dust at the air temperature above 18°C.

DISEASES

Powdery Mildew

White powdery growth on the leaves. The infected leaves rot.

Control: Spray sulphur-based fungicides like lime-sulphur, wettable sulphur, Sulfex, Sulphatox etc.

Downy Mildew

The affected parts looks like wet cotton and slimy. The affected part rots immediately.

Control: Spray Dithane M-45(2g/L)

Anthracnose

Circular spots develop on fruits or stems. The affected branch dries and fruits drop. Control : Spray Dithane M-45 (2g/L), Blue copper (3g/L) and Difoltan (2g/L) alternately at a week interval.

Black spot

The infected leaves show brown or black spots. They expand and the leaves rot.

Control: Spray Dithane M-45(2g/L) twice or thrice at an interval of 10-15 days.

Dieback

It is considered a menace to rose and citrus culture. It has no remedy. But the preventive measures are very useful. Grow healthy plants with improved cultural methods and ward off the trouble. Week plants are easily infected with dieback due to malnutrition, disease and insect attacks. Chlorosis, black spot, thrip or scale insect infestation etc. make the plants week and are indirectly related to dieback. The abundance of healthy foliage over the entire period of the growing season makes the plants stronger to resist the trouble. The plant should not suffer from the want of micronutrients.

Control: The foliar application of micronutrients twice in a growing season is recommended. While pruning the knife blade should be sterilized with spirit at short intervals.

Gummosis

The bark cracks and a gum-like substance exudes. Scrape the infected area and apply Bordeaux paste over it.

Control: Blilox or Blue Copper (50g/L) can also be applied at a week interval for 2-3 times.

Canker

The citrus fruits especially the limes are attacked by this disease. The hot and humid weather favours the spread of the disease. The infected part looks rusty. The heavily infected branches dry out. The plants suffering from malnutrition are very susceptible to this disease.

Control: Spray Bordeaux mixture and streptocyline (1g/50L) alternately. Soak *neem* cake in water. Spray the solution thrice at a week interval.

Conservatory for Bonsai

The bonsai is acclimalised to a semi-shade condition. Hence the significance of the term 'Indoor Bonsai'. The sun of the tropics is very strong which should be reduced artificially for the slow growth of the plants. In winter however, the full sun is enjoyed by both the deciduous and evergreen bonsai. For March to October the bonsai should be reared in the conservatory. Generally a lean to the house conservatory is constructed. Now-a-days for making a conservatory agro-shade netting is available in the market.

Manufacturers/Dealers.

1. B & V Agro Irrigation Co.
   410 AGH Chambers, 379/81 Narshi Nath Street,
   Kath Bazar Masjid, Bunder, Bombay-9.

2. Creative polymers.
   2500/18, G.I.D.C.Industrial Estate,
   P.O.Halol, Dist. Panchmahal, Gujrat,
   Pin-389350.

3. Doulatram Agro-tech Pvt. Ltd.
   B-40, Sanjay Building, No.5 Mittal Ind. Estate,
   Andheri-Kurla Rd. Mumbai, Pin-400059.

4. Tulip Garden Shop
   E-2/61 Arera Colony
   Bhopal, Pin-462016.

It makes the construction very easy with minimum of the maintenance cost. The plastic netting is spread over a bamboo structure. Both the canopy and the walls are made of the plastic netting. Obviously the size of the shed should be such as to accommodate a number of pots to be housed therein. In the dry and hot summer noon the bonsai should be treated like the indoor plants in regard to providing a humid environment. The conservatory can be kept moist by opening a sprinkler at an hour's interval in the peak period of the driness.

A conservatory can be constracted by using bamboo or wooden laths. Bamboo mats or coconut leaves can also be used with advantage. A creeper may be used for this purpose. It is trained over a pergola which serves as the canopy of the house.

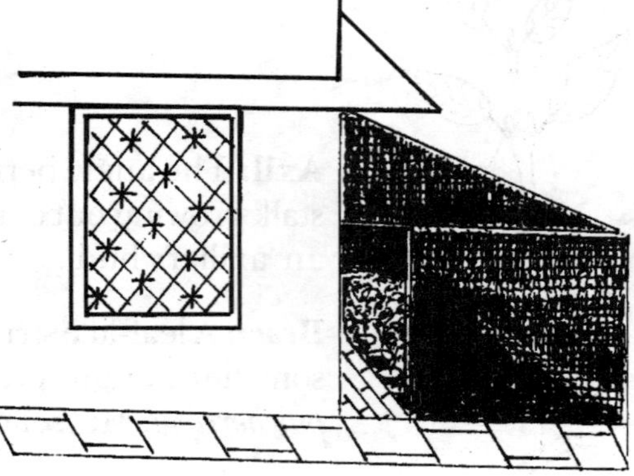

Fig. 137: *Lean-to-wall conservatory made of agro-shade netting*

Glossary

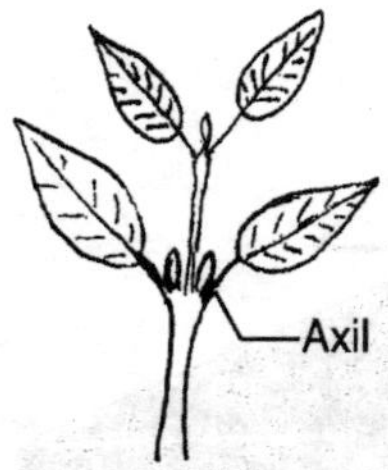

Axil: The angle between the stem of a plant and the leaf stalk growing out of it. A bud growing in this angle is called an 'axillary bud'.

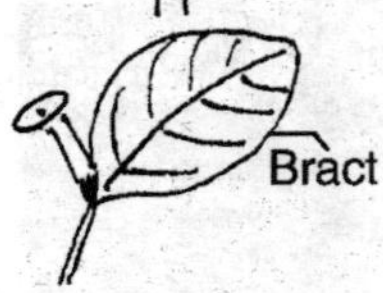

Bract: A leaf-like structure which subtends a flower bunch, sometimes brightly coloured and petal-like, e.g. in *Euphorbia pulcherrima*, Mussenda etc.

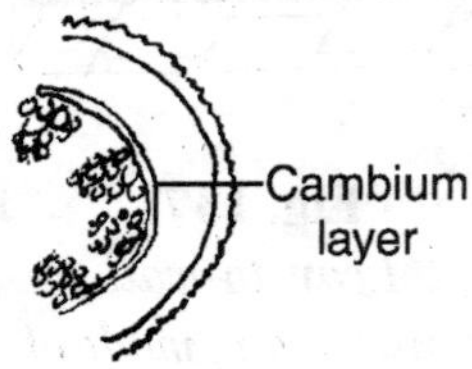

Cambium layer: The living cells lying just beneath the bark of a tree and at the growing tips of roots and shoots.

Deciduous: The trees and shrubs which shed their leaves entirely in winter, e.g. *Bombax malabaricum*.

Dicot : The abbreviated term of dicotyledon. The plant bearing two cotyledons or seed leaves.

Disbudding : The removal of the bud especially the side shoots and surplus buds to force the plant to concentrate its energies in the remaining single bud.

Evergreen : A plant having leaves that remain green and functional throughout the year. The old leaves fall sparingly.

Herb : Any non-woody vascular plant. The secondary growth in thickness which is the characteristic of a woody plant does not take place.

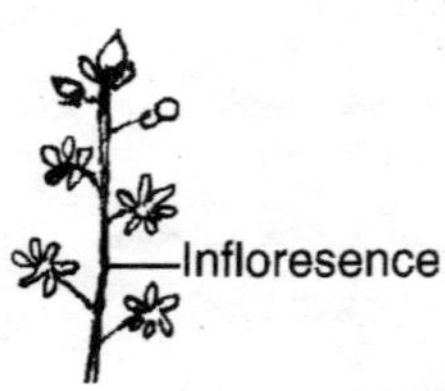

Inflorescence: The flowering part of a plant, individual florets of a group comprising a flower head.

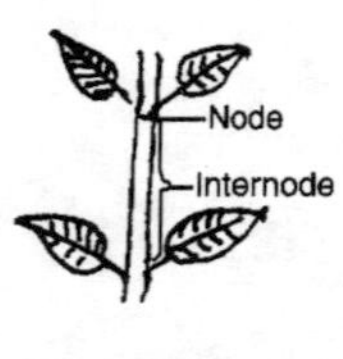

Internode : The portion of the stem of a plant lying between two adjacent leaf joints (nodes).

Lamina: The blade of a leaf or petal usually thin, large and leathery.

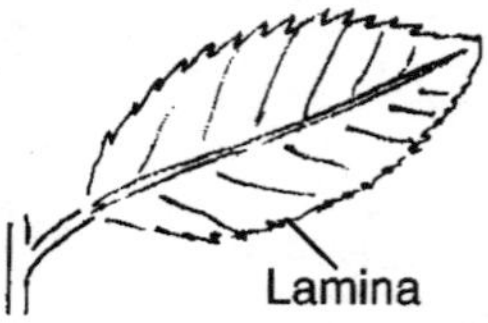

Leaflets: The small leaf-like components of a compound leaf.

Linear: Describing leaves that are slender and elongated.

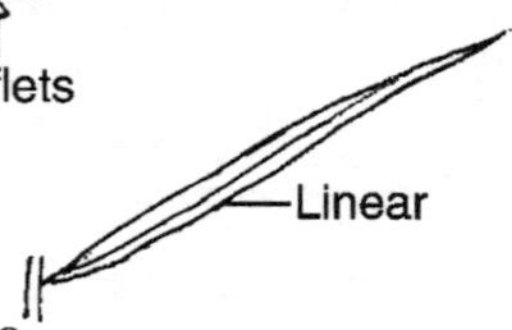

Loam : Soil having even proportions of clay (including silt) and sand.

Monocot : The abbreviated term of monocotyledon. The plant having one cotyledon or seed leaf.

Perennial: A plant that lives for many years

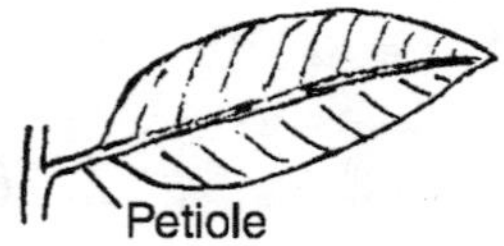

Petiole : The stalk that attaches leaf blade to the stem.

Prop root : Any adventitious root that arises from the stem to provide additional support to the plant, as a banyan tree.

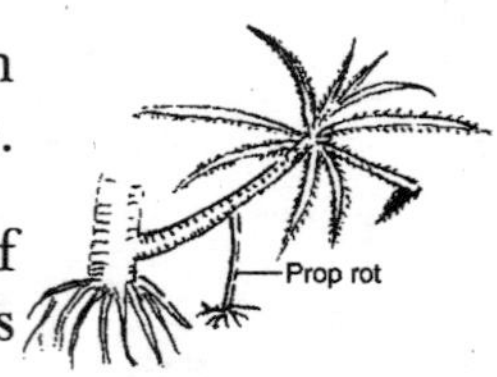

Runner : A creeping branch that arises from the base of the plant and runs along the ground. The roots and plantlets may arise at nodes (leaf joints).

Sepal : A part of a flower, usually at the base of the flower protecting the petals, often like a small leaf.

Serrate, Serrated : Applied to leaf margins notched like a saw with forward-facing teeth.

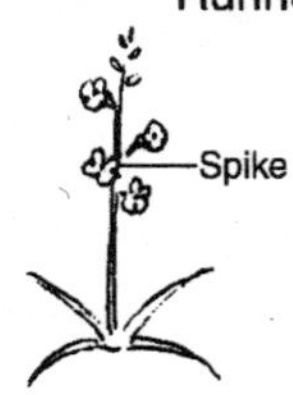

Shrub : A loose term often used to describe a relatively short-growing woody plant producing shoots from the base and a number of stems, not a tree-like single stemmed plant.

Spike : A long axis having stalkless flowers.

Stamen: The male (pollen producing) part of a flower consisting usually of filament and anther (pollen bag).

Stilt root : Same as prop root

Sucker : An adventitious shoot that develops from the root and runs a distance under the ground.

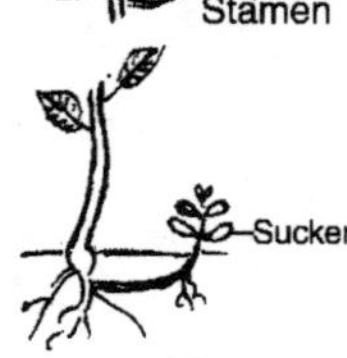

Bonsai Nursery

(Dealing in bonsai or planting materials for bonsai)

1. Sameer Priya Nursery
   Sugandh, 126 New Colony, Shop No.4
   Nagpur, Pin 440001.

2. Green Nursery and Florists
   9, Pakhowal Road, Ludhiana,
   Pin-141001.

3. Minerva Nursery
   Chandi, Diamond Harbour Rd,
   P.O. Bishnupur, Dist. 24 Parganas (S),
   Pin 743503.

4. Bangasree Nursery
   Diamond Harbour Rd, P.O. Bishnupur,
   Dist. 24 Parganas(S), Pin-743503.

5. B.R.Pandit Studio Pottery (dealing in bonsai pots)
   Kalakar Niwas, Panchal Udyog Nagar,
   Goddev Pathak Rd., Bhayandar(E)
   Thane, Pin-401105.

6. Sri Eswara Farm and Nursery
   Burilanka, East Godavari (A.P.)
   Pin 533126

7. Plants Land
   6-3-1104, Somajiguda, Raj bhavan Rd.
   Hyderabad, pin 500082.

8. Sri Sai Ram Nursery
   1-10-72, Beside Suryodaya buildings
   Begumpet, Hyderabad, Pin 500016

9. Samak Farms and Nurseries
   5, C.S.C. DDA Hauz khas, New Delhi Pin 110016.

10. The Nilgiri Seed Depot
    P.B.24, 51-E/2 Ettinners Rd.
    Ootacamund, (T.N.) Pin 643001.

11. Pathare
    46-51, Shankar Nagar, Durg,
    Pin 491002 (M.P.)

12. Empress Garden Nursery
    Near Race Course, Pune, Pin 411001.

13. Horticultural Arena (For banyan seedlings)
    (Authors's Nursery) KadamKanan, Jhargram,
    Midnapore, Pin 721507.

14. Rock Garden Nursery
    Opp. Glaxo, Worly, Mumbai-25.

15. Shyama Bhagwati Nursery
    Peragrasswala Compound,
    S No. 111, Opp. Manish Nagar, Near Four
    Bungalows, J.P.Rd, Andheri(W), Mumbai-58.

16. Kedia Nursery
    Singhu Border, G.T.Karnal Rd, Delhi, Pin 110042.

ENGLAND

1. Bourne Bridge Nurseries
   Oak Hill Rd., Staplford Abbotts, Romford, Essex.

2. Bromagi and young
   Wild Acre, Brookhurst Road, Cranleigh, Surrey.

3. Dawn and Peter Chan Bonsai
   9 Riddles down Avenue, Purely, Surrey.

4. Greenwood Gardens
   Ollerton Road, Arnold Notts.

5. Middle Earth Bonsai
249 Lytham Rd., Southport, Merseyside.

6. Tokonoa Bonsai, 14 London Rd.
Shenly, Rodlett, Herts.

7. Potters Garden Bonsai
The Boat House, Potters Lane, Samlesbury, Preston.

8. Price and Adams, Cherry Trees
22 Burnt Hill Road, Wrecelesham, Surrey.

9. Adreanne Weller
St. Mary's Garden, Worplesdon, Surry.

Bonsai Societies

ENGLAND

1. Bedfordshire Bonsai Society, 65, Richmond Hill, Luton, Beds LU 27JG
2. Bristol Bonsai Society, 35 Clevedon Rd, Finland, Bristal, Avon.
3. British Bonsai Association, 23 Nimrod Road, Streatham, London SW 16.
4. Croydon Bonsai Club, 7 Mulberry Lane, Croydon, Surrey CRO 6QR
5. Japan Society of London Bonsai, Kai, 39 West Square, London SE 1145P.
6. Manchester Bonsai Society, 160 Cheadle Old Road, Edgerley, Stockport, Cheshire.
7. Middlesex Bonsai Society, 54 Tregenna Avenue, Harrow, Middx HA 28QS
8. National Bonsai Society, 24 Bidston Rd. Liverpool L47XJ
9. National Bonsai Society, 98 Fairfield Rd. Burgess Hill, Sussex RH158NT
10. Yorkshire Bonsai Association, 187 West Park Drive West, Leeds W. Yorks LS82BE

AUSTRALIA

1. Victoria Bonsai Association, 14 Sussex Street, Brighton 3186.
2. Bonsai in Australia, 14 New Hall Avenue, Moonic Ponds, 3939, Australia.
3. National Bonsai Association, C/o 22 Burraga Avenue, Terrey Hills, NSW 2084, Australia.

BELGIUM

1. European Bonsai Association, Groenstraat 28, B-9170 Waasmunster, Belgium.

FRANCE

1. Club Parisienne De Bonsai, 29 Rue Du Roi De Sicilie, 775004, Paris, France.

ITALY

1. Bonsai Clubs D' Italia, Str. Mongreno 3411032 Torino, Italy.

JAPAN

1. Kawaguchi Bonsai Association, 2-1-1 Aoki, Kawaguchi City, Saitame-Pref. Japan.

LUXEMBURG

1. Bonsai Club Luxembarg, 4, Cite Kennedy, L-7234 Walferdage.

SOUTH AFRICA

1. Shibui Bonsai Kai, P.O.Box 81084, Parkhurst, 2120 South Africa.

SPAN

1. Association Espanola De Bonsai, Pasco de la Pechina 15, Valencia-8.

SWITZERLAND

1. Scheizer Bonsai Liebhaberclub, Capuzinerweg 8, CH 6006 Luzeru, Switzerland.

USA

1. Bonsai Institute of California, P.O.Box 78211, Los Angeles, CA 90016-1211, USA.

1. Bill M. Valavanis, 412 Pinnacle Rd. Rochester, NY 14623.

GERMANY

1. B.C.Verein Europaischer M, Postfach 106209 6900, Heidelburg. Germany.

2. Lesniewicz, Manneheim Strats 401, 6900, Heidelburg, W. Germany.

INDIA

1. Indian Bonsai Society, Mrs L. Jhaveri, 105 Samundra Mahal, Dr. Annie Besant Road, Worli, Mumbai.

2. Bonsai Study Group of the Indo-Japanese Assoc., Oricon House, 7th Floor, 12 Rampart Road, Mumbai 400023.

Reading Materials

1. Indoor Bonsai – Paul Lesniewicz
(Blandford Press, Dorset)

2. Wonderworld of Tropical Bonsai-Jyoti and Nikunj Paresh (Vikils, Feffer and Simons Ltd., Mumbai-1)

3. Bonsai Culture-Leila Dhanda
(Oxford & 1B1 Publishing Co. Delhi-1).

4. Bonsai For Beginners
(Ratanshi Velji Shah, Mumbai-27)

5. Bonsai – Harry Tomlinson
(Dorling Kindersley Ltd, London)

6. Successful Bonsai Growing – P. Adams

7. An Introduction to Bonsai
(Gallery Books, 112 Madison Avenue, Newyork-10016).

8. A guide to Bonsai – Peter Chan
(Bracken Books Ltd. London).

9. Bonsai With American Trees – Masakuni
(Kadansha International Ltd. Newyork).

Index

(Species and Cultivars)

Index

(GENERAL)